1707

The Union of Scotland and England

This book is due for return on or before the last date shown below.

Don Gresswell Ltd., London, N.21 Cat. No. 1208   DG 02242/71

1707

The Union of Scotland and England

in contemporary documents
with a commentary

P. H. Scott

Published in association with the Saltire Society

CHAMBERS

Note

I have previously developed some of the points made in the commentary in a number of separate essays and articles: on bribery, Andrew Fletcher's idea of union and military intimidation in *The Scotsman* of 10 September 1977, 15 April 1978, and 29 April 1978; on Sir Walter Scott's attitude to the Union and on Defoe in *Blackwood's Magazine* of September 1976 and October 1977; on Scott again in *Q* of September 1976 and 5 November 1976; and on the role of Hamilton in a radio talk broadcast by the BBC Radio Scotland on 12 February 1978.

First published by W & R Chambers Ltd Edinburgh 1979

ISBN 0 550 20265 X

Printed in Great Britain by
T & A Constable Ltd Edinburgh

CONTENTS

The procession and sitting of the Scottish Parliament,
from a French engraving of c1680.

(Reproduced from the collection
of the Scottish National Portrait Gallery.)

'We shall esteem it as
the greatest glory of our reign.'

*Queen Anne's message to the
Scottish Parliament, 3 October 1706*

'That most obnoxious of measures—
the Union of the Kingdoms.'

Sir Walter Scott
Introduction to Rob Roy

Introduction

British parliaments have often disregarded, or in effect modified, the provisions of the Treaty of Union of 1707. Even so the constitutional arrangement which the Treaty established between Scotland and England has survived in its essentials.

Meanwhile many other things have changed drastically: not least the role and functions of government. For about a hundred years the Constitution of 1707 (for that is what it amounts to) has come increasingly under criticism. This has now reached the point where a substantial body of opinion in Scotland is in favour of constitutional change. The obscurities and confusions of the Referendum of March 1979 are unlikely to be the last word on the subject. There is therefore now more reason than ever that we should try to understand what it is that we are proposing to change. What happened in 1707 and why?

By any standard, the Union was one of the most important events in our history. In Scotland, only the War of Independence and the Reformation had such long-lasting and far-reaching consequences. Politically, and in many other ways, it has been the dominant factor in our affairs for more than 250 years. From the English, and indeed from the European and world, point of view its results have also been far from trivial. By freeing England from concern with the Border in the north, and pooling the resources of the two kingdoms, it enabled the new creation, Great Britain, to become for about the same period a great European and Imperial Power.

One might expect that an event of such importance, and one so full of drama and excitement, would have been studied and analysed until there was little more to say. In fact, this is not so. There are very few books on the subject, and most of them, with one recent exception—William Ferguson's *Scotland's Relations with England: A Survey to 1707* (John Donald, 1977)—are inadequate and misleading. English historians have usually been indifferent to Scottish affairs and content that the Union seemed to have disposed of them. For the Scots, the subject was at first too painful. 'By a kind of unconscious instinct', Hume Brown wrote, 'Scotsmen have deliberately averted their gaze from a reign so momentous in their country's destinies, and abounding, moreover, in men of striking gifts and individuality.'* In a book written for children, *The Tales of a Grandfather*, Sir Walter Scott provided a robust and realistic account at the beginning of the last century. His lead was not followed. With a curious kind of historical prudery, 19th-century and some later historians have deliberately obscured the realities. The dominant Whig school of historians required to fit the Union into an account of irresistible constitutional progress and they could do this only by suppressing much of the evidence. Under this influence, the Union became almost sacrosanct. It was regarded as something both inevitable and desirable which should not be questioned too closely.

There is, in fact, a great deal of hard evidence. Three of the people involved in the action were writers of exceptional talent. Andrew Fletcher of Saltoun, who played a leading part in the opposition to the Union in the Scottish Parliament, was a political thinker of originality and penetration. Another member of the Parliament, George Lockhart of Carnwath, wrote *Memoirs* which are pugnacious and illuminating. On the other side was no less than Daniel Defoe, a propagandist of genius long before he was a novelist. He was sent to Edinburgh as an English agent and wrote copiously, for both private and public consumption, including a *History of the Union* in 800 pages folio. There was a 'pen and ink war' of pamphlets. Above all, many hundreds of letters from the central figures in the struggle have survived, even many that were intended to be kept secret. Most of these men were intelligent and articulate. They knew what was happening and expressed it vividly. We hardly need to speculate when the written records are so full and so clear. The majority of these letters were published in a number of collections during the 19th century; but these books, and even those of Fletcher, Lockhart and Defoe, are now very rare.

For such reasons as these, A. C. Davis of the Saltire Society suggested that I might put together a collection of extracts from contemporary documents to illustrate the controversies surrounding the Union, on similar lines to one which the Society had already published on the Reformation. I readily agreed to do this because I had long been pursuing these documents in the British Museum and the National Library of Scotland with increasing astonishment that they were not better known and that the obvious conclusions had not been drawn from them. It soon became clear

* The Legislative Union of England and Scotland *(1914) page 5*

to me that it would be insufficient to confine the extracts to the public controversy, which had less effect on events than other causes, but that the material could be arranged chronologically to show how the crisis developed. The result is something between a source book, a narrative and a commentary. I have included some quotations from more recent writers when they have something particularly cogent to add to the discussion.

In several respects, the view of the Union which emerges differs from the accepted theories, but it is one which seems to me to flow irresistibly from the evidence. The conventional idea is that the Union of Parliament in 1707 was a logical development of an association between the two countries which had been growing steadily closer since the Union of the Crowns in 1603. In fact, the experience of the association was unsatisfactory in the extreme to the Scots and caused them to seek more, and not less, independence. Similarly, much of the discussion in Scotland before 1707 about closer union or a treaty meant something very different from the arrangement eventually made. The importance of considerations of trade in bringing about the Union has been greatly exaggerated. On the other hand, few accounts have admitted the extent to which the Scottish Government, and the negotiators of the Treaty, were puppets of the English Court. Many historians have denied the clear evidence of bribery, and it seems that no one has previously suggested that bribery is also the most probable explanation for Hamilton's sabotage of the opposition. Little emphasis has been placed on military intimidation or the fear of civil war, although most contemporary accounts suggest that these considerations were the strongest argument for the Union.

In the space available, this is inevitably a mere sketch of a very complex matter. It tells the story essentially from the Scottish point of view. Many details, side-issues and sub-plots are omitted. Some important points are mentioned in a few brief sentences. I hope, however, that there is sufficient substance, especially in the extracts from the original sources, to give a fair picture of the way in which the Union came about, and to encourage further enquiry.

ONE

The Nature of the Crisis

The Union of 1707 was one of several possible responses to a crisis in the relationship between Scotland and England, although not the solution which either side really wanted. It was a crisis with deep roots. In 1603 James VI of Scotland, on the death of Queen Elizabeth of England without any direct heir, had succeeded also to the English throne. He left his smaller kingdom to live in the larger, creating a constitutional problem without precedent. At a time when kings had very real, if not absolute, power, James was simultaneously the Head of two States which had long been not only separate and independent, but hostile. How were they to adjust to this new situation?

It was a problem which had been foreseen at the time of the marriage in 1503 between James IV of Scotland and Margaret Tudor (the daughter of Henry VII of England) by virtue of which James VI eventually inherited his right to the English throne. At the time, some of Henry's advisors saw the possibility that the marriage might lead to the rule of a Scottish King in England. Henry told them not to worry. Such an event 'would be an accession not of England to Scotland, but of Scotland to England, since the greater would always draw the less, as England had drawn Normandy under her sway'. Events quickly proved that Henry had been right.

James's own immediate response to the problem was to seek to merge all the institutions and practices of the two separate kingdoms into one. This was consistent with his ideas of absolute monarchy; but he made little progress, beyond giving the two countries, by royal prerogative alone, the joint name of Great Britain. When this attempt at merger failed, James's policy was to use the wealth and power of the larger country to impose his will on Scotland. This worked reasonably well in his own lifetime. He was in a strong position. In both countries he was the executive head of the government and all state appointments were at his disposal. For the Scots, he was a native Scottish king who understood the country intimately and spoke its language, and was unlikely to disregard its well-being.

As long as he remained King, the system of absentee manage-ment was tolerable.

His successor Charles I, who was educated in England, attempted the same policy but met only with rebellion. By 1641 Scotland had established Presbyterianism in defiance of the King and, in advance of England, had asserted the freedom of the Scottish Parliament from royal control. These achievements, however, were insecure as long as the risk remained of the King using English power against them. The Scots sought to reduce the risk by intervention in the English Civil War on the Parliamentary side. They did not want to destroy the Monarchy but to curb it. They hoped that the danger of royal interference with religion would be reduced if England adopted, as they had in fact promised in the Treaty of the Solemn League and Covenant, a similar church settlement to the Scottish. They realised that Scottish trading and security interests would be disregarded if the King remained free to conduct foreign policy and make war on English advice alone. They therefore sought some arrangement with England under which these matters would be subject to joint control. (To the confusion of subsequent historians they called such an alliance or loose federal structure a 'Union'; which was a perfectly natural use of the word at the time.) The English never seriously entertained any such ideas, and any prospect of them was swept away by Cromwell, who simply annexed Scotland by military force.

This temporary incorporation was abandoned, evidently with relief on both sides, when the monarchy was restored in 1660. But, at the same time, the Scottish Parliament lost the freedom which it had asserted successfully in 1641. Scotland was back where it was before the revolution against Charles I. The absentee King, with his policy influenced and interpreted by English officials, ruled the country through the Privy Council and a controlled Parliament. All state appointments were made from London. The Scottish administration appointed in this way was a puppet of the English Court. Foreign policy was a royal prerogative. 'The Sovereign', Macaulay wrote, 'even if he had the wish, had not the power, to bear himself evenly between his large and his small kingdoms, between the kingdom from which he drew an annual revenue of a million and a half and the kingdom from which he drew an annual revenue of little more than sixty thousand pounds. He dared neither to refuse his assent to any English law injurious to the trade of Scotland, nor to give his assent to any Scotch law injurious to the trade of England.'

Scotland, in consequence of the shared monarchy, was automatically involved in the continental wars undertaken by England in her own interests, but which were destructive of the traditional pattern of Scottish trade. In an age of intense and exclusive commercial rivalry backed by naval power, England regarded Scotland as a rival and discriminated against her in the Navigation Acts. England grew in power and wealth; Scotland, deprived of the means of economic self-defence, and already devastated by the civil wars, sank into abject poverty.

There was a flicker of hope in 1688 when the flight of James VII and II brought William to the throne, under conditions separately negotiated by the two Parliaments. In the Scottish case, Parliament threw off the royal shackles re-imposed in 1660. From then until 1707, the Scottish Parliament was once again a real force. It still had to accept the appointment by the King in London of the officers of state who formed the Scottish Government; but laws could not be passed, nor finance raised, without a majority vote in Parliament. The Government was powerless to carry out the policies required by its masters in London, unless it could somehow, by persuasion or other means, obtain the votes. Parliament could not only resist and frustrate the policies of London, it could formulate and demand alternatives of its own. It was clearly an unstable arrangement; but at least Scotland once again had an instrument to make her views felt.

Inevitably, the Scottish Parliament turned to measures designed to restore Scottish trade from the effects of a century of neglect and discrimination. In 1695 it passed an Act for a company trading to Africa and the Indies. This was the Company of Scotland, which, as the first of its ventures, decided to settle a colony at Darien. William as King of Scotland gave his assent to the Act and signed the Charter of the Company. As King of England, he was obliged to do all he could to sabotage and oppose the efforts of the Company. His English Government prevented the raising of capital in London and on the Continent and issued proclamations throughout the Colonies to deny trade or support of any kind to the Scottish Company. The capital was raised in Scotland alone in an astonishing effort of national fervour, requiring most of the disposable wealth of the country. When the Darien scheme failed it was largely due to mismanagement and inadequate preparation but the constitutional anomaly had not helped. How could a country succeed when its own Head of State actively opposed its interests? England also had been made aware of the problem, because the efforts of the Scottish

Company were not only a challenge to their trading monopolies but a complication of their foreign policy. Darien had made it obvious that the dual monarchy would not work and that some drastic revision of the constitutional arrangement was inescapable.

At this critical moment, when relations between the two countries were as bad as they had ever been, a dynastic accident offered a solution. The last possible direct heir of Queen Anne died in 1700. In 1701, the English Parliament, without consultation with Scotland, passed the Act of Settlement, passing the succession after Anne to the Electress Sophia and her descendants, the so-called Hanoverian Succession. Scotland was in no way bound by this decision. She was therefore free, at least in theory, either to break the Union of the Crowns by deciding on a different successor, or to make her acceptance of the Hanoverian Succession conditional on limitations of the royal prerogative which would stop English interference in Scottish affairs.

On one point, opinion in Scotland was virtually unanimous: the misery to which the country had been reduced was a consequence of the removal of the King to London in 1603 without any constitutional safeguards for Scottish interests. Among others, Andrew Fletcher of Saltoun in his pamphlets and speeches explained the reasons, as in this speech to Parliament in 1703:

'My Lord Chancellor,   *3*
When our kings succeeded to the crown of England, the ministers of that nation took a short way to ruin us, by concurring with their inclinations to extend the prerogative in Scotland; and the great places and pensions conferred upon Scotsmen by that court, made them to be willing instruments in the work. From that time this nation began to give away their privileges one after the other, though they then stood more in need of having them enlarged. And as the collections of our laws, before the union of the crowns, are full of acts to secure our liberty, those laws that have been made since that time are directed chiefly to extend the prerogative. And that we might not know what rights and liberties were still ours, nor be excited by the memory of what our ancestors enjoyed, to recover those we had lost, in the two last editions of our acts of parliament the most considerable laws for the liberty of the subject are industriously and designedly left out. All our affairs, since the union of the crowns, have been managed by the advice of English ministers, and the principal offices of the kingdom filled with such men, as the court of England knew would be subservient to their designs: by which means they have had so

visible an influence upon our whole administration, that we have, from that time, appeared to the rest of the world more like a conquered province, than a free independent people. The account is very short: whilst our princes are not absolute in England, they must be influenced by that nation; our ministers must follow the directions of the prince, or lose their places, and our places and pensions will be distributed according to the inclinations of a king of England, so long as a king of England has the disposal of them: neither shall any man obtain the least advancement, who refuses to vote in council and parliament under that influence. So that there is no way to free this country from a ruinous dependence upon the English court, unless by placing the power of conferring offices and pensions in the parliament, so long as we shall have the same king with England. The antient kings of Scotland, and even those of France, had not the power of conferring the chief offices of state, though each of them had only one kingdom to govern, and that the difficulty we labour under, of two kingdoms which have different interests governed by the same king, did not occur. Besides, we all know that the disposal of our places and pensions is so considerable a thing to a king of England, that several of our princes, since the union of the crowns, have wished to be free from the trouble of deciding between the many pretenders. That which would have given them ease, will give us liberty, and make us significant to the common interest of both nations. Without this, it is impossible to free us from a dependence on the English court: all other remedies and conditions of government will prove ineffectual, as plainly appears from the nature of the thing; for who is not sensible of the influence of places and pensions upon all men and all affairs? If our ministers continue to be appointed by the English court, and this nation may not be permitted to dispose of the offices and places of this kingdom to balance the English bribery, they will corrupt every thing to that degree, that if any of our laws stand in their way, they will get them repealed. Let no man say, that it cannot be proved, that the English court has ever bestowed any bribe in this country. For they bestow all offices and pensions; they bribe us, and are masters of us at our own cost. It is nothing but an English interest in this house, that those, who wish well to our country, have to struggle with at this time. We may, if we please, dream of other remedies; but so long as Scotsmen must go to the English court to obtain offices of trust or profit in this kingdom, those offices will always be managed with regard to the court and interest of England, though to the betraying of the interest of this nation, whenever it comes in competition with that of England. And what less can be expected, unless we resolve to expect miracles, and that greedy, ambitious, and for the most part necessitous men, involved in great debts, burdened with great families, and having great titles to support, will lay down their places, rather than comply with an English interest in obedience to the prince's commands? Now, to find Scotsmen opposing this, and willing that English ministers, for this is the case, should have the disposal of places and pensions in Scotland, rather than their own parliament, is matter of great astonishment; but that it should be so much as a question in the parliament, is altogether incomprehensible: and if an indifferent person were to judge, he would certainly say we were an English parliament. Every man knows that princes give places and pensions by the influence of those who advise them. So that the question comes to no more than, whether this nation would be in a better condition, if, in conferring our places and pensions, the prince should be determined by the parliament of Scotland, or by the ministers of a court, that make it their interest to keep us low and miserable. We all know that this is the cause of our poverty, misery and dependence. But we have been for a long time so poor, so miserable and depending, that we have neither heart nor courage though we want not the means, to free ourselves.'

That Fletcher did not exaggerate the subservience and dependence of the holders of 'the principal offices of the Kingdom' is apparent from their surviving letters to English Ministers. The Earl of Glasgow, for instance, wrote as follows to the English Lord Treasurer, Godolphin, on 14 June 1705:

'My Lord,—The honor you did me in your last in letting me know *4* the justice your Lop. was pleased to doe me in reading my letter to the Queen, vindicating me from that aspersion of counteracting her Majesties measures last sessions, and that her Majesty was satisfied the same was a misrepresentation, hath made me perfectly easy; for I had rather chosen death then acted so humorous and base a part; and must acknowledge my self infinitely bound to your Lop. for your goodness, and shall ever retain a gratefull sense of it, and shall most faithfully and heartily serve your Lop. if ever providence give me ane occation, bot, alas, I fear I never have ane opportunity to testifie my duty and gratitude, bot, whill I breath, I ever shall have the good will; and I am known never to be worse then my word.

B

And now, my Lord, that your Lop. hath been instrumentall in procuring me this mark of her Majesties favor in naming me her Treasurer-Deputt, I am truly out of countenance, and know not what returns to make your Lop. I give you my humble and hearty thanks, and begs leave to give your Lop. all the assurances of a man of honor that I ever will faithfully and sincerly serve her Majesty to the uttmost of my power, and, whatever measures the Queen pleaseth to goe in to, either in this or any other session of Parliament, I shall heartily comply with without reserve or in the least disputing her commands. And, whatever sett of persons the Queen shall find necessar to bring in to her government, I shall chearfully concurr with them, for I bless God I have exceptions against no man the Queen can prevail with to serve her interest. And, my Lord, I shall also with ten tymes greater satisfaction lay doun my post when her Majesty finds it convenient for her service then I now accept of it, and serve her Majesty faithfully so far as I have access in my private station. My Lord, I have my oun fears that the Queens affairs shall not have the wished for success, bot I shall be glad to be disappoynted.

My Lord, I from my heart wish your Lop. all health and happiness, and that your Lop. may ever continue in the honorable post you now enjoy shall be the constant and earnest prayer of, may it please your Lop., etc.,

Glasgow.'

In the most famous of his pamphlets, *An Account of a Conversation concerning a right regulation of Governments for the Common Good of Mankind*, Fletcher described the economic consequences of the constitutional anomaly. In this extract, 'I' is Fletcher himself, and 'Sir Edward' is Sir Edward Seymour, a member of the English Parliament:

5   'I said we are an independent nation, though very much declined in power and reputation since the union of the crowns, by neglecting to make such conditions with our kings, as were necessary to preserve both: that finding, by experience, the prejudice of this omission, we cannot be justly blamed for endeavouring to lay hold on the opportunity put into our hands, of enacting such conditions and limitations on a successor, upon the expiration of the present intail, as may secure the honour and sovereignty of our crown and kingdom, the freedom, frequency, and power of our parliaments, together with our religion, liberty, and trade, from either English or foreign influence. Sir Edward

all in a fret; hay day, said he, here is a fine cant indeed, independent nation! honour of our crown! and what not? Do you consider what proportion your bear to England? not one to forty in rents of land. Besides, our greatest riches arise from trade and manufactures, which you want. This was allowed by me: but I desired to inform him, that the trade of Scotland was considerable before the union of the crowns: that as the increase of the English trade had raised the value of their lands, so the loss of our trade had sunk the rents in Scotland, impoverished the tenant, and disabled him, in most places, from paying his landlord any other ways than in corn; which practice has been attended with innumerable inconveniences and great loss: that our trade was formerly in so flourishing a condition, that the shire of Fife alone had as many ships as now belong to the whole kingdom: that ten or twelve towns, which lie on the south coast of that province, had, at that time, a very considerable trade, and in our days are little better than so many heaps of ruins: that our trade with France was very advantageous, by reason of the great privileges we enjoyed in that kingdom: that our commerce with Spain had been very considerable, and began during the wars between England and that nation; and that we drove a great trade in the Baltic with our fish, before the Dutch had wholly possessed themselves of that advantageous traffic. Upon the union of the crowns not only all this went to decay, but our money was spent in England, and not among ourselves; the furniture of our houses, and the best of our clothes and equipage, was bought at London: and though particular persons of the Scots nation had many great and profitable places at court, to the high displeasure of the English, yet that was no advantage to our country, which was totally neglected, like a farm managed by servants, and not under the eye of the master. The great business both of Scots and English ministers was, to extend the prerogative in Scotland, to the ruin of liberty, property, and trade: and the disorders, which were afterwards occasioned by the civil war, gave the last and finishing blow to the riches and power of the nation. Since that time we have had neither spirit, nor liberty, nor trade, nor money among us.'

Fletcher was by no means alone in this diagnosis. To give only one example from the opposite side, Daniel Defoe, who was sent to Edinburgh in 1706 by the English Government as a spy and propagandist to help to overcome Scottish resistance to the Union, said in his *History of the Union Between England and Scotland*:

6   'The Scots had been very sensible of the visible decay of trade, wealth and inhabitants in their country, even from the first giving their Kings to the English succession; and, as the sinking condition of their nation was plainly owing to the loss of their court, concourse of people, the disadvantages of trade, and the influence the English had over their Kings; so, it was as plain, there was no way to recover themselves, but either better terms of Union and Alliance, or a returning back to their separate self-existing State . . . for Scotland was . . ., in a political though not in a legal sense, always under the management of the English Court, . . . it had the subjection without the advantages.'

From the Scottish point of view, therefore, the simple acceptance of the English *fait accompli* of the Hanoverian Succession was not an option. If there was one thing which the history of the last hundred years had proved beyond doubt it was the need for some arrangement to overcome the disadvantages of the Union of the Crowns, which had given the Scots 'subjection without the advantages'. They had lost control not only over foreign policy and the making of war and peace, but even over the appointment of quite minor officials, judges and officers, and the disposal of revenue raised in their own country. Their trade had been destroyed and could not be restored as long as their own government was under the control of their monopolistic neighbours. The Scots had missed the opportunity of the 'Glorious Revolution' of 1688 when they accepted a change of monarchy without adequate safeguards. They did not propose to make the same mistake again.

TWO

The Act of Security

In the 18th century, parliaments everywhere were representative of only a small part of the population. In Scotland, the three estates of nobles, and Commissioners of the Shires and the Burghs, sat together in one House. The nobles were, of course, hereditary. In the shires only a handful of lairds with a restrictive property qualification had the right to vote in elections, and only the self-perpetuating body of magistrates in the burghs. Many of the lairds and magistrates were clients of one of the great lords. The last such Parliament was elected in May 1703, and continued until it dissolved itself by approving the Treaty of Union in January 1707. During the whole of this time, it was preoccupied with the critical problem of the relationship with England. It was a struggle which fell into two phases: a period of determination to assert Scottish independence, from May 1703 to September 1705, and the collapse of resistance after that, leading to the approval of the Treaty in January 1707.

The first phase was dominated by the ideas of Andrew Fletcher, and it was of this period that George Ridpath wrote, 'the memory of this Parliament will be precious to the Nation, so long as it has a being'. Fletcher argued that there were only two possible solutions to the constitutional anomaly which had deprived Scotland of independent action and subjected her to the control of the English Court. Either a separate successor to the Throne should be chosen to follow Queen Anne, or, if the same successor were accepted, 'limitations' to the royal prerogative should be applied to ensure the transfer of effective power to Parliament. These limitations provided for annual parliaments, which would make all appointments to places and offices, have the right of decision on peace and war and all treaties, and pass legislation from which royal assent could not be withheld.

This entire programme was too republican in spirit to be accepted by the majority as it stood, but the essential principles were embodied in the Act of Security approved in 1703. This provided that in the event of the death of the Sovereign without a lawful heir:

8   'the foresaid Estates of Parliament Conveened or Meeting are
hereby Authorized and Impowered to Nominat and Declare the
Successor to the Imperial Crown of this Realme and to settle the
succession thereof upon the heirs of the said successors body;
The said successor and the heirs of the successors body being
allwayes of the Royal line of Scotland and of the true protestant
Religion Provideing allwayes that the same be not successor to
the Crown of England unless that in this present Session of
Parliament or any other Session of this or any ensueing Parliament
dureing her Majesties reign there be such conditions of Government settled and enacted as may secure the honour and sovereign-
ity of this Crown and Kingdom, the freedom frequency and
power of Parliaments, the religion liberty and trade of the Nation
from English or any foreigne influence With power to the said
Meeting of Estates to add such further conditions of Government
as they shall think necessary. . . .
And for a further Security of the Kingdom Her Majestie with
advice and consent foresaid Statutes & Enacts That the whole
Protestant Heretors and all the Burghs within the same shall
furthwith provide themselves with fire arms for all the fencible
men who are Protestants within their respective bounds.'

In 1703 Royal assent to the Act was withheld on instructions
from London. For the next session the Officers of State were
re-shuffled in the hope of regaining control; but when Parliament
again insisted on the Act, assent was conceded by the English
Minister, Godolphin, and it became law in 1704. The Scottish
Parliament had defiantly asserted its independence.

But, of course, that was not the end of the matter. In the
first place, the choice of a separate successor would involve risks
within Scotland itself. The ejection of the last Stuart King in 1688
had given security to Presbyterianism and restricted arbitrary
Royal power. A Stuart successor might again challenge them,
backed both by Jacobites in Scotland and by France. The
requirement in the Act of Security that the successor must be of
the 'true protestant Religion', was intended to provide against
this risk. The safer course might be the second of the alternatives,
the Hanoverian succession as in England, but with constitutional
arrangements to safeguard the independence of the Scottish
Parliament. The real difficulty was that England was prepared
to accept neither. Any assertion of Scottish independence involved
the risk of the revival of the alliance with France, with which
England was at war. A Scottish Parliament liberated from indirect

English control, even with the same King, involved the possibility of disturbance of English foreign policy and trade of the kind already experienced over Darien.

Somehow Scotland had to be kept in the subordinate position to which the Union of the Crowns had reduced her, more by accident than design. Jonathan Swift put the point succinctly:

'. . . it was thought highly dangerous to leave that Part of the *9* Island inhabited by a poor, fierce Northern People, at liberty to put themselves under a different King . . . and so the Union became necessary, not for any actual Good it could possibly do us, but to avoid a probable Evil; . . . the most considerable Person of the adverse Party, and a great Promoter of the Union, [Lord Somers, a leading Whig political manager] frankly owned to me, that this Necessity, brought upon us by the wrong Management of the Earl of Godolphin, was the only cause of the Union.'

Or, as Sir John Clerk of Penicuik put it in an essay to justify his vote for the Union:

'It was absolutely against the interest of England to suffer Scotland *10* to grow rich in a separate state because it was more than probable that this increase of wealth would sometime or other be made use of to the prejudice of England. (Long animosities between the two nations made this so very probable that it had been perfectly chymerical to have thought otherways.)'

THREE

The English Reaction

The English response to the challenge of the Scottish Act was rapid; it is described in the *Parliamentary History*:

11 'On the 9th [January 1705], the Lords presented an Address to the queen, importing, "That, having taken into consideration divers acts of parliament lately passed in Scotland, and duly weighed the dangerous and pernicious effects which were likely to follow from them, they were preparing bills for preventing such great evils; and, in the mean time, they thought themselves bound to represent to her majesty, as their humble opinion, that it was highly requisite for the safety of this kingdom, that speedy and effectual orders be given for putting of Newcastle into a condition of defence, for securing the port of Tinmouth, and for repairing Carlisle and Hull. They also besought her majesty to cause the militia of the 4 northern counties to be disciplined and provided with arms and ammunition; and a competent number of regular troops to be kept upon the northern borders of England and in the north parts of Ireland: and to direct the laws to be effectually put in execution against all papists in respect to their arms and persons, and to order a particular account of what was done, in execution of her commands, to be laid before her majesty in counsel without delay."

To this Address the Queen answered, "That she should direct a survey to be made of the several places mentioned in this Address, in order to lay it before the parliament: And what forces could be spared from their attendance here, should be quartered upon the borders, as they had been the last year: And that she would likewise give the necessary directions upon the other particulars of the Address."

The Commons likewise, having in a grand committee, considered the State of the Nation with regard to Scotland, resolved on the 18th of December, that a "Bill should be brought in for the effectual securing the kingdom of England from the apparent dangers, that might arise from several acts lately passed in the parliament of Scotland."

And on the 11th of January, Mr. Conyers reported from the committee of the whole House, to whom it was referred to consider of heads for that bill, the Resolutions they had to come to, and which were as follow:

"That it be one head of the bill to enable her majesty to nominate and appoint commissioners for England to treat with commissioners from Scotland, for an Union between the two kingdoms. 2. That all natives of the kingdom of Scotland, except such as are settled and shall continue inhabitants of England, or the dominions thereunto belonging, or at present in the service of the army or navy, shall be reputed as aliens, unless the succession to the crown of Scotland be settled on the princess Sophia of Hanover and the heirs of her body being protestants. 3. That a more effectual provision be made to prevent the exportation of wool from England and Ireland into Scotland. 4. That provision be made to prevent the importation of Scots linen into England or Ireland, and to permit the exportation of the linen manufactures of Ireland in English bottoms into her majesty's plantations in the West-Indies. 5. That immediate provision be made to prevent the conveying of horses, arms, and ammunition, from England into Scotland. 6. That all the protestant free-holders of the six northern counties of England be permitted to furnish themselves with arms."

These Resolutions being read twice, all, except the last, were agreed to by the House, who appointed a committee to prepare and bring in a bill accordingly; . . . On the 1st of February, the Commons read it a third time, and passed their own bill relating to Scotland; and the following Christmas was the day prefixed for the Scots to enact the succession, or, on failure thereof, then this act was to have effect.'

'It was', wrote Defoe of the Act, 'the most impolitic, I had   *12* almost said unjust, that ever passed that great assembly.'

This was an ultimatum threatening an economic blockade and hinting at the possibility of military action. The Act mentioned the possibility of Union; but (contrary to the account of most historians) the ultimatum related not to this but to Scottish acceptance of the Hanoverian Succession. In fact, for the whole of the first phase of the crisis, this was the first objective of the English Government and the solution which they would have preferred. They wished to preserve unchanged the system which had given them indirect and concealed control of Scottish affairs, and therefore did everything possible to press the Scottish Parliament to accept the Succession. Queen Anne's instructions in April 1704 to Seafield as Lord Chancellor of Scotland were quite specific:

13   '1. Anne R. Instructions to our right trusty and right well-beloved cousin and councellor, James, Earle of Seafield, our Chancellor. You are to repair to Scotland without loss of time and there make knowen our pleasure that wee are fully resolved to doe all that in us lyes to have the succession setled failing airs of our body on Princess Sophia of Hannover and the airs of her body, and that wee will imploy none in our service but such as will concurr in so necessary and so good a worke. 2°. In order to the compassing of this wee doe hereby impower you to give to men of quality and interest such assurances of our favour as you shall judge necessary. And wee, reposing intire trust in you, are resolved to make these assurances good. And this you may shew as your credentiall, but doe it only where the shewing of it is absolutely necessary to create a confidence in you. Given att our Court att Saint James's, the 5th day of Aprile, 1704, and of our reign the 3d year. A. R.'

The same document, incidentally, illustrates the methods of the Royal management of Parliament:

'As to the lords and gentlemen of qualitie and interest that are averse to the succession, you are to leat them know from us that the speedie setling of it in Scotland is indispensablie necessarie for the peace and queit of our reigne in al our dominions, and that we will take their complyence and submission to our pleasur in this mater for ane unquestionable proofe of ther dutie and affection to us, and as to such of them as you cannot prevail with to concurr, you are to endeavour at least to soften them in their opposition, or to get them to be absent.

Bot notwithstanding the præceeding instruction, and that without further loss of time you may have some men of interest to go in heartilie with the commissioner and you in your deliberations, and the pains that are immediatlie upon your araival to be taken with the members, you are, as soon as the Earles of Rothes and Roxburgh and Mr. Bailie of Jerveswood declair themselves free and willing to ingadge in our measurs, and not till then, to let them know that we are resolved to make the Earle of Rothes governour of our Castel of Edinburgh, or to provid him other-wayes in such maner as that he shal be satisfyed, and the Earle of Roxbourgh our secretarie, and Mr. Bailie of Jerveswood our thræsurer depute; bot as to the time of declairing them, befor the session or after, you are to advise with the commissioner and transmitt his judgment and yours to us.'

Seafield in his correspondence with Godolphin, a leading member of the English Government, continually emphasises that he understands that Succession was the preferred solution. On 8 June, 1705, for example:

'My Lord,—This packet caries the draught of the instructions for the Commissioner and draught of the letter to the Parlament. They are proposed either for a treatie or the present setelment of the succession, as her Majestie shal think fit to determin. I know the succession is most desirable, bot I am verie afraid it will not succeed at this time, and manie of her Majesties most faithful servants and who heartilie wish the setelment of the succession are of this opinion, and, if it fails, it will be a præjudice to it, and I am affraid give great strenthe and advantage to the opposing pairtie, wheras that of a treatie seems more probable to succeed, bot as for my selfe I shal chearfulie obey her Majesties commands, as I have alreadie done in this last Parlament in this mater.'

Little over a month later, on 18 July 1705, Seafield reported failure to Godolphin. The Scottish Parliament stubbornly refused to accept unconditional succession. They adopted a Resolve repeating, in effect, the essential points of the Act of Security:

'Resolved that this Parliament will not proceed to the nomination of a successor till wee have had a previous treatty with England in relation to our commerce and oy^r concerns with that nation; and, further, it is resolved that this Parliament will proceed to make such limitations and conditions of government for the rectificatione of our constitution as may secure the liberty, religion, and independancie of this kingdome before they proceed to the said nomination.'

Seafield commented:

'The Comm^r has called sēralls of the Servants this day, and wee all aggreed that there remains nothing now to be done concerning the succession in this session of Parliament, and that wee ought to endeavour to have ane act for a treatty in such termes as that wee might hope to have some success. So wee are to try what influence wee can have upon the members of Parliament for obtaining ane act for a treatty, leaving the nomination to the Queen, and, if we cannot prevail in that, to joyn that there be a good nomination. If this cannot carry, wee will be necessitat to bring the session to a close as soon as wee can.'

It was only at this stage, after the frustration of three years of constant pressure to bring Scotland into the same Succession to the Throne, that the English Government decided to go for the alternative, a Treaty to determine the relationship between the two countries. Godolphin wrote to Seafield on 23 July in a tone of resignation:

17   'My Lord, finding by the honour of your lordship's of the 18th that the settlement of the succession is postpon'd to a previous treaty, the next thing desirable is that such an Act for a treaty may bee prepared as the Queen may pass. For certainly no body can be surprized when the Parliament will not settle the succession if the Queen refuses her royall assent to any Act for a treaty that shall be clogged with restrictions and diminutions of that little power which is yett left to the Crown.

The sincerity of those who pretend to be friends to a treaty will easily appear in this point; for unless they are content such an Act should goe single and upon its own foot, it will be very plain that at the bottom their design is only to obstruct what they pretend to bee for.

Such an Act as this, with some maintenance for the forces, and a speedy end of the sessions, is what the Queen is still willing to flatter herself may be obtained. But if it can not, the sooner she know it I think the better for her service.'

Seafield replied on 1 August:

18   'My Lord,—My Lord Comm^r and I receaved yor Lo^{ps} letter, whereby you signifyed to us that, in respect the Parliament had by a resolve postponed the setlement of the succession to a treatty, that, therefor, we should use our endeavours to obtain such ane act of treatty as her Ma^{ty} could give her royall assent to. Wee did, in conjunction with the Duke of Queensbery, use our outmost endeavours to prepare the members of Parliament for this, and I spoke to above fourscore of them myself that had been for the resolve, and found a great many of them well inclyned to a treatty.'

A Treaty, of course, did not necessarily mean a Union of the kind eventually concluded. The Scottish Parliament was evidently thinking, in terms of the Resolve of July 1705, of a Treaty which established a satisfactory relationship with England in matters of trade and other common concerns but secured their independence. There had indeed been talk of Union much earlier than this and even negotiations, but the initiative and the pressure had always come from the Monarch, for whom life would be easier if he could treat his two kingdoms as one. It began in fact with James VI and I who made the point in his picturesque language in a speech to the English Parliament in March 1603:

'What God hath conjoined let no man separate. I am the husband and the whole isle is my lawful wife; I am the head and it is my body; I am the shepherd and it is my flock. I hope therefore that no man will think that I, a Christian King under the Gospel, should be a polygamist and husband to two wives; that I being the head should have a divided or monstrous body or that being the shepherd to so fair a flock should have my flock parted in two.' *19*

Towards the end of the century, William and then Anne resumed the pressure; but they met with little response. An attempt at negotiations in 1702 and 1703 simply petered out and was abandoned with relief by both sides. Neither country liked nor trusted the other. 'Never two nations', wrote Defoe, 'that had *20* so much affinity in circumstances, have had such inveteracy and aversion to one another in their blood.' Or, as the 19th-century English historian, James Anthony Froude, expressed it: 'The *21* English hated Scotland because Scotland had successfully defied them: the Scots hated England as an enemy on the watch to make them slaves. The hereditary hostility strengthened with time, and each generation added fresh injuries to the accumulation of bitterness.' Neither country had their hearts in the idea of closer association. To the Scots, it looked like the revival in another form of the secular English attempts to assert supremacy. The English, in the confidence of superior wealth, were reluctant to open their door to a flood of beggarly Scots. Their attitude was summed up in the words which Fletcher attributes to the English Parliamentarian, Sir Edward Seymour: 'What a bother is here *22* about a Union with Scotland, of which all the advantage we shall have, will be no more than what a man gets by marrying a beggar; a louse for her portion?'

In the same pamphlet, *An Account of a Conversation* (1703), Fletcher remarks, 'I have observed, that a treaty of union has *23* never been mentioned by the English, but with a design to amuse us when they apprehended any danger from our nation. And when their apprehensions were blown over, they have always shewn they had no such intention.' The apprehension became acute in 1705 and the English Government, for the first time, set about the achievement of Union in real earnest.

FOUR

Divergent Ideas of Union

If a Treaty did not necessarily mean Union, neither did the word 'union' mean the same thing to both sides, or to everyone involved in the controversy. Since 1707 the word has acquired, in this context, a quite specific meaning; but this was not so in the period immediately before the Treaty was concluded and ratified. Many of the strongest opponents of the Treaty consistently argued for 'closer' or 'more perfect' union, but by this they meant something quite different from the fusion of the two Parliaments. They were in fact using the word (as the examples in the Oxford English Dictionary demonstrate) in accordance with its general usage up to that time, as meaning the opposite of discord and conflict, or any form of association for any common purpose. The word certainly could mean joining one thing with another so as to form one complete whole; but in this sense the word had normally been used only in a religious or metaphysical context. Disregard of this semantic point has bedevilled a good deal of the subsequent comment on the controversies of 1703 to 1707.

Some historians, for example, have thought that Fletcher was being inconsistent or had changed his mind because he both wrote of the need to 'unite' with England and strenuously resisted the Treaty of Union. In fact, he constantly advocated both without inconsistency and explained quite clearly what he meant. In his *Account of a Conversation* he argued that not only Scotland and England but countries throughout Europe should form associations to reduce the risk of 'bloody and destructive wars', but that other forms of union would involve 'the miserable and languishing condition of all places that depend upon a remote seat of government'. Countries should co-operate to encourage industry and contribute to their joint security and defence, but their relationship should be one of equality. 'This is the only just and rational kind of union. All other coalitions are but the unjust subjection of one people to another.'

Fletcher developed the distinction at length in his pamphlet, *State of the Controversy betwixt United and Separate Parliaments* (1706). The purpose of this was to argue strongly against the dissolution of the separate Scottish Parliament; but, at the same time, he was in favour of closer union, in the sense in which he used the word:

'It is certainly the Interest of all Good Men to promote a nearer Union with our Neighbours of England; and no time ought to be lost on our part in going about so good a Work.'

25

He added, nevertheless:

'. . . in the most Absolute and Incorporate Union that can be made betwixt these two Nations, there are several Interests (and of the greatest Consequence too) which are and must be reserved separate to each Nation . . . it seems beyond humane comprehension, how these separate distinct Interests, and Establishments, can be regulated and supported by one Parliament . . . for the Scots to subject these Interests to an United Parliament is so far from being an expedient to avoid English Influence, that it is the way to throw themselves head-long into it; and the Scots deserve no pity, if they voluntarily surrender their united and separate Interests to the Mercy of an united Parliament, where the English shall have so vast a Majority. . . .'

'I shall close what I have to say, touching this Dream of being one and not two, by putting the Case, That a Law were offered in the united Parliament, (to make it go down the better) and that it were brought in by one of the 45 Scots Members, for some Regulation in the Church-Government, or for some Regulation of the Civil Judicatures, or touching some matters of Trade; and supposing, that whatever smooth Title this Law might have, yet it did point at no less than to over-turn the Church, or Civil Judicatures in *Scotland*, or to ruine the Trade of *Scotland*; I suppose the other Scots Members should oppose this Law, as being prejudicial to the Scots Rights reserved in the Articles of Treaty; The Answer is very ready and plain, That there is no such thing as Scots or English, they are all British, they are one, and not two; the Law now proposed cannot hurt the Scots no more than the English; if it does hurt, it does hurt to the British, of which the English are a part; and the only way to know whether it does hurt or good to the British, is to put it to the Vote of a British Parliament.

This will be the Issue of that darling Plea, of being one and not two; it will be turned upon the Scots with a Vengeance; and their 45 Scots Members may dance round to all Eternity, in this Trap of their own making.'

So remote was the proposal for an United Parliament from the sort of Treaty which the Scots had in mind, that Fletcher thought that such a proposal was likely to destroy the possibility of any agreement at all:

26   'it is known to every Body, that many of the greatest and wisest Men of this Nation are absolutely against an United Parliament, as a measure most likely to frustrate the Treaty.'

James Hodges, in his book, *The Rights and Interests of the Two British Monarchies* (1703), argued the case for federalism, which he defined:

27   'A Confederate or Federal Union is that, whereby Distinct, Free, and Independent Kingdoms, Dominions or States, do unite their seperate Interests into one common Interest, for the mutual benefit of both, so far as relates to certain Conditions and Articles agreed upon betwixt them, retaining in the mean time their several Independencies, National Distinctions, and the different Laws, Customs, and Government of each.

Concerning which, we are to consider, That the word Union in this Federal Sense, is a general Term of a very large Comprehension, tho' restrain'd to the amicable Compacts, Relations, and Obligations of Kingdoms and States to one another.'

He argued that an Incorporating Union would mean the 'irrecoverable Ruin' of Scotland, but would not be in the interests of England either because it would be unjust and therefore unstable:

'The *English* are to retain their Distinct Soveraignty, Independent State, and National Privileges and Dignity after the same manner as they did before enjoy them, with what Addition the Accession of *Scotland* can make; whereas all these Benefits are lost to *Scotland* and engross'd by *England* in an *Incorporating Union*.

For in so far as by its Effects here recited, it contradicts the first Fundamental Rule of *Union* mention'd in the first Argument, That an *Union* of Both must be Founded in the Interest of Both, it can never be contrary to the Interest of the One but it must also be contrary to the Interest of the Other, seeing thereby in a large measure it frustrates the Concord, Security, good Understanding, and the mutual Satisfaction, Service, and Assistance, which are amongst the chief Effects of a Happy *Union*, and disposeth to Repining, Grudging, Resentment, Division, Separaration [sic], Devising, and Pushing on intestine Commotions, and Rebellions, and Encouraging Assaults from Foreign Enemies, which are amongst the principal Effects of an Unhappy *Union*, which that by Incorporating is here suppos'd and prov'd to be.'

The Scottish Parliament so much approved of James Hodges 'who hath in his writings served the interests of this Nation', that they passed a resolution on 10 August 1705, granting him a reward of 4800 pounds Scots.   28

That these ideas were widespread in Scotland is apparent from the addresses against an Incorporating Union which flooded into the Scottish Parliament from all over the country. The General Convention of the Royal Burghs, for example, in their Address of 29 October 1706, said that they were 'not against an honourable and safe Union with England, consisting with the Being of the Kingdom and Parliament thereof', but they petitioned against an Incorporating Union,

'by which our Monarchy is supprest, our Parliaments extin-   29
guished, and in consequence our Religion, Church Government, Claim of Right, Laws, Liberties, Trade, and all that is dear to us, daily in danger of being encroached upon, altered, or wholly subverted by the English, in a British Parliament, wherein the mean representation allowed for Scotland can never signify in securing to us the Interest reserved by us, or granted to us, by the English. . . .'

At least one man in Scotland took a contrary view from the beginning and, like a precursor of the 'Scotland is British' campaign, objected to the mere existence of the names Scotland and England. This was the Earl of Cromartie, who wrote to Mar on 1 January 1706:

'On this New Year Day, many happy years are wished by me (and   30
I am sure by many Scotsmen) to yow and your family; and (as that which I think Scotland's cheeff politick good) to ane intire union with England. I doe not mean without provisions and exceptiones—that were ridiculous for both—but in substantials, that both head and body might be one politick body. Unless wee be a part each of other, the union will be as a blood puddin to bind a catt; and till one or the other be hungry, and then the puddin flyes. God give all of yow prudence, wisdome and honesty and Brittish minds. May wee be Brittains, and down goe the old ignominious names of Scotland, of England. Scot or Scotland are words not known in our native language. England is a dishonorable name imposed on Brittains by Jutland pirats and mercinaries

C

to Brittains, usurping on their lords. Brittains is our true, our honorable denomination.'

There is no evidence that anyone else in Scotland thought like this at the time, and it is questionable if anyone in England ever has.

Although Hodges and others described these ideas as federal, it is apparent from their arguments that they were thinking of a much looser arrangement than is usual in federal constitutions. They envisaged the continued existence of two independent countries, sharing the same king, co-operating over defence and foreign policy, with trading relations regulated by Treaty; but neither interfering in the internal affairs of the other. They were arguing for more, and not less, real independence than Scotland had in fact enjoyed since 1603.

These ideas met with a blank rejection in England. Mar wrote from Whitehall to William Carstares in Edinburgh on 9 March 1706. (Carstares had been an advisor on Scottish affairs to King William. He was now Principal of Edinburgh University, Moderator of the General Assembly and actively engaged in overcoming the resistance of the Kirk to the Union.)

31   '. . . they [the English negotiators] tell us plainly, they will give us no terms that are considerable for going into their succession, if any, without going into an entire union; and, if we insist upon that, they will never meet with us; for they think all the notions about foederal unions and forms a mere jest and chimera. I wrote this freely to you, though it is not fit this should be known in Scotland, for fear of discouraging people, and making them despair of the treaty. You see that what we are to treat of is not in our choice, and we see the inconveniences of treating an incorporating union only.'

FIVE

Religion, Liberty and Trade

The Act of Security had set out the Scottish objectives: the security of their sovereignty, of Parliament, and of religion, liberty and trade, 'from English or any foreign influence'.* Sovereignty, Parliament and freedom from English influences were all abandoned when the Treaty of Union was accepted. What were the consequences for religion, liberty and trade, and to what extent did they determine the outcome?

The Earl of Roxburghe was one of the leaders of a group in the Scottish Parliament known as the *Squadrone Volante*. Originally they supported Fletcher but finally, after complicated negotiations in London, switched to acceptance of the Union. Roxburghe was raised to a dukedom after 1707. There is a well-known passage in one of his letters in the *Jerviswood Correspondence*:

'The motives will be, Trade with most, Hanover with some, ease   *32*
and security with others, together with a generall aversion at
civill discords, intollerable poverty, and the constant oppression
of a bad ministry, from generation to generation, without the
least regard to the good of the country. . . .
. . . whatever the inconveniences on't may be, such as quitting a
name and a poor independent sovereignty to Scotland, for a small
share in a great one, and degradation to Scotch nobility, (for
election is that), yet the risque, or rather certainty, of the Prince
of Wales, in case of Union's failing, and the forenamed advantages
in case of it's succeeding, have their weight.'

The first part of this, 'trade with most', is often quoted, as though it were a final judgement on the question, to prove that trade was the decisive issue. But even in the tortuous syntax and logic of this passage, the worry about the 'Prince of Wales', which means the Jacobite Succession, is apparent. In fact, in his agonised efforts to decide the balance of advantage to his country, his party and himself, Roxburghe in the course of this correspondence veers about between almost every possible point of view. Elsewhere, for

* *See extract 8.*

33   instance, he says that a Treaty 'is destruction for Scotland', and elsewhere again that the alternative to Succession or a Union was
34   military conquest by England 'upon the first Peace'. (In other words, as soon as Marlborough's armies were disengaged in Europe.) He is much more concerned with these political questions than with trade, which he does not mention again in the whole correspondence.

Other advocates for the Union set out their own list of advantages. This is Seafield's:

35   'My reasons for conjoining with England on good termes were these: that the kingdome of England is a Protestant kingdome and that, y'for, the joyneing with them was a security for our religion. 2°, England has trade and other advantages to give us, which no other kingdome could affoord; 3°/, England has freedome and liberty, and that the joyning with it was the best way to secure that to us; and 4°/, that I saw no other method for secureing our peace, the two kingdomes being in the same island, and forreign assistance was both dangerous to ourselves and England and that, y'for, I was for a treatty.'

Once again trade is mentioned, but there is more emphasis on 'religion and liberty'. From the English side, Lord Somers in a letter to the Earl of Marchmont pleading for his support for the Union, has a similar list which does not mention trade at all:

36   'The establishing the Protestant religion, the setting the succession, the fixing the monarchy, the securing the liberties of the people and setling peace throughout the Island, are matters of such moment as I hope will never be thrown away for a humour or upon any private consideration.'

The opponents of the Treaty argued that its effects on Scottish
37   trade would be positively harmful. 'Free Trade with England in an Incorporating Union must be the inevitable Ruin of Trade in Scotland,' concluded Hodges, and Fletcher agreed with him:

38   'I am of opinion, said I, that by an incorporating union, as they call it, of the two nations, Scotland will become more poor than ever.
Why so?
Because Scotsmen will then spend in England ten times more than now they do; which will soon exhaust the money of the nation. For besides the sums that members of parliament will every winter carry to London, all our countrymen, who have plentiful

estates, will constantly reside there, no less than those of Ireland do at this time. No Scotsman, who expects any public employment, will ever set his foot in Scotland; and every man, that makes his fortune in England, will purchase lands in that kingdom: our trade, which is the bait that covers the hook, will be only an inconsiderable retail, in a poor, remote, and barren country, where the richest of our nobility and gentry will no longer reside: and though we should allow all the visionary suppositions of those who are so fond of this union; yet our trade cannot possibly increase on a sudden. Whereas the expences I mentioned will, in a very short time, exhaust us, and leave no stock for any kind of commerce. But, said the Earl [Cromartie], you do not distinguish right, nor consider where the fallacy of your reasoning lies. You talk of Scotland and Scots money, and do not reflect, that we shall then be a part of Britain; England will be increased by the accession of Scotland, and both those names lost in that of Britain: so that you are to consider the good of that whole body, of which you then become a citizen, and will be much happier than you was, by being in all respects qualified to pretend to any office or employment in Britain, and may trade or purchase in any part of the island. But, by your leave, my lord, let me distinguish plainly, and tell you, that if I make a bargain for the people that inhabit the northern part of this island, I ought principally to consider the interest of those who shall continue to live in that place, that they may find their account in the agreement, and be better provided for than they are. For if the advantages of getting employments, trading and purchasing in any part of the island, are the only things to be considered, all these may be as well obtained by any one who would change his country in the present state of things. And if, in the union of several countries under one government, the prosperity and happiness of the different nations are not considered, as well as of the whole united body, those that are more remote from the seat of the government will be only made subservient to the interest of others, and their condition very miserable. On the other hand, besides our fishery, which God and nature has given us, together with the great privileges already granted to our African company, a distinct sovereignty does always enable a people to retain some riches, and leaves them without excuse if they do not rise to considerable wealth. So that if a sufficient provision be made to prevent the exhausting of our money by the attendance of Scotsmen at court, and to take away the influence of English ministers upon our affairs, no condition of men will be more happy. For we shall then be possessed of liberty; shall administer our own affairs, and be free from the corruptions of a court; we shall have the certain and constant alliance of a powerful nation, of the same language, religion, and government, lying between us and all enemies both by sea and land, and obliged in interest to keep perpetual peace and amity with us. And this you cannot but allow to be a much happier condition, than any we ever could propose to ourselves by all the projects of union that have hitherto been formed. Here the Earl endeavoured, by many arguments, to shew, that our country would be the place, where all manufactures, as well for the use of the whole island, as for exportation, would be made, by reason of the cheapness of living, and the many hands that Scotland could furnish. I said the contrary was not only most evident, but that the union would certainly destroy even those manufactures we now have. For example, the English are able to furnish us, at an easier rate, with better cloth than we make in Scotland: and it is not to be supposed they will destroy their own established manufactures to encourage ours. . . . But sure you will allow, said the Earl, that a free commerce with England, and the liberty of trading to their plantations, which cannot be expected without an union, must be of incomparable advantage to the Scots nation, . . . I cannot see [,said I] what advantage a free trade to the English plantations would bring us, except a farther exhausting of our people, and the utter ruin of all our merchants, who should vainly pretend to carry that trade from the English. The Earl, who knew the truth of these things, was unwilling to insist any longer upon this ungrateful subject; and therefore, proceeding to another argument, said, that when we shall be united to England, trade and riches will circulate to the utmost part of the island; and that I could not be ignorant of the wealth, which the remotest corners of the north and west of England possess. . . . I desired him to consider, that Wales, the only country that ever had united with England, lying at a less distance from London, and consequently more commodiously to participate in the circulation of a great trade than we do, after three or four hundred years, is still the only place of that kingdom, which has no considerable commerce, though possessed of one of the best ports in the whole island; a sufficient demonstration that trade is not a necessary consequence of an union with England.'

The English propagandist, Defoe, had an almost mystical faith in the glories of trade, but even he had doubts about the economic effects of the Treaty in Scotland. When he was writing for an English audience, he could assure them that the Union would bring them a new market, 'a new and vast Ocean of Wealth and Trade shall be laid open in the North'. In his pamphlets in Scotland he valiantly argued the converse while the debate was still open; but when it was safely over, he too fell back on religion and liberty:

39

'Whatever loss some may allege Scotland suffers in this Union, in matters of commerce, in removing her parliaments, in lessening the conflux of her nobility and gentry to Edinburgh, in taxes, and in carrying away her people, things which time may remedy and repay her for with interest; yet this the most prejudiced man in Scotland must acknowledge they have in exchange, and which, if they know how to value it, is worth all they have paid or can pay for it; I mean Liberty in its due and best extent, religious and civil.'

40

Not only the theorists and propagandists had misgivings about the effects on trade. The Convention of Royal Burghs was the body most representative of the trading community. Their Address against the Union, after the passage already quoted*, went on to say:

'And by these articles our Poor People are made liable to the English taxes, which is a certain unsupportable burden, considering that the trade proposed is uncertain, involved, and wholly precarious, especially when regulate as to export and import by the laws of England, and under the same prohibitions and restrictions, customs, and duties; and considering, that the most considerable branches of our Trade are differing from those of England, and are and may be yet more discouraged by their laws; and that all the concerts of Trade, and our Interest, are, after the Union, subject to such alterations as the Parliament of Great Britain shall think fit. . . .'

41

In talking, as the Act of Security did, of securing the trade of the Nation 'free from English or any foreign influence', or aiming, in the words of the Resolve of 1705, at a treaty in 'relation to our commerce and other concerns with that nation',† the Scottish Parliament evidently had some commercial objectives in mind. We do not know precisely what these were because there was never any negotiation on this basis. They presumably wanted some assurance that the Company of Scotland would be free to trade without English interference or opposition. They may have

---

* See extract 29. † See extracts 8 and 15.

sought some relaxation in the English Navigation Acts which restricted trade with the Colonies to English ships. They certainly wanted access to the English market for Scottish cattle and linen, the main export trade since the disruption of Scotland's traditional trading links with continental Europe. On the other hand, there were strong disadvantages in the arrangements introduced by the Treaty of Union which exposed the poorer country to unrestricted competition by the wealthier and introduced a system of taxes and duties designed for English conditions. The trade provisions of the Treaty were therefore a very mixed blessing and unlikely by themselves to persuade Scotland to accept the Treaty, if she had been left to make a free choice.

The religious aspect was equally ambivalent. When Seafield spoke of 'security for our religion', he meant that the ejection of James VII and II and the accession of William had established Protestantism by removing a King who had inclinations towards the restoration of Catholicism. The implied argument was that the best way to protect this settlement was to adhere to the same Protestant Succession as England. 'The Union', wrote Defoe, 'is a mountain thrown on the grave of the late King James and his Roman Posterity, which covers them so deep, as that all their Party will never be able to dig them up again.' A return to a separate Scottish King, even of 'the true protestant Religion' (in the words of the Act of Security), involved the danger of a Jacobite revolt, backed by France, and a return to the religious and dynastic wars of the 17th century. The trouble was that the established churches in Scotland and England were poles apart in structure and doctrine. Presbyterianism in Scotland had been defended at great cost in blood and effort against repeated attempts at assimilation from south of the Border. What security would the Church of Scotland enjoy, if the country became subject to a British Parliament in which England, and therefore Episcopalianism, had an overwhelming majority, and which included a House of Lords, of which Bishops were members by virtue of their office? The whole idea was repugnant to the spirit, and indeed the letter, of the Covenants.

The Scottish Church was therefore exposed to a cruel dilemma. They saw the force of the argument about the Jacobite risk, but was this a lesser danger than assimilation in an Episcopalian England? During the debate on the Treaty, aversion to this assimilation was so strong that the extremes met and Presbyterian and Jacobite joined in common opposition to the Union. 'It was plain,' wrote Lockhart of Carnwath, 'such a desperate

Disease required a desperate Remedy.' Mar reported to London: 'One thing I must say for the Kirk, that if the Union fail it is oueing to them.' Defoe agreed: 'The most dangerous rock of difference, on which this Union could split, and which could now render it ineffectual, was that of religion.'

On 12 November 1706, in an attempt to appease Presbyterian misgivings, the Scottish Parliament passed an Act of Security for the Church, guaranteeing that it would 'continue without any alteration to the people of this land in all succeeding generations.' (The same Act, incidentally, also guaranteed the survival of the four universities.) The Act was to be regarded as an indissoluble part of the Treaty, and to be subscribed and sworn to by all succeeding monarchs at their accession. This stratagem did something to reduce the heat of opposition by the Church at the critical moment, but it did not eradicate it. Defoe's chief activity as an English agent, and probably his most important contribution to the Union cause, was among the clergy. He could claim to have been bred as a Presbyterian himself, and even to have suffered in the pillory and prison for his faith. 'They take me for their Friend', he reported to Harley, '. . . I am in the Morning at the Committee, in the Afternoon in the assembly. I am privy to all their folly, I wish I could not call it Knavery, and am Entirely Confided in.' But even six months after the Treaty had been accepted by the Scottish Parliament, Defoe realised that the Church had not been reconciled to it. He wrote to Harley on 10 June 1707: 'I am Travailing thro' the Towns and Disputeing with The Rigid and Refractory Clergy who are the worst Enemies of the Union.' With religion, as with trade, there was therefore no unambiguous and undisputed advantage in the Union.

What then about 'liberty'? It is plain that when advocates for the Union, like Seafield, Somers or Defoe, spoke about this, they meant something very different, even the opposite, from the original objectives of the Scottish Parliament. The Act of Security had sought to protect the power of the Parliament from English influence; the Treaty proposed to abolish the Scottish Parliament altogether and to create a British Parliament in which England would have an overwhelming majority. Seafield and the others were using the word, in close relation to the religious question, to mean freedom of the risk of arbitrary royal rule, which might have followed from a restoration of the Stuarts. They were, in effect, asking the Scottish Parliament to make a complete *volte-face*, and abandon the objectives which they had repeatedly confirmed since the beginning of the crisis.

44
45

46

47

48

There was, however, another risk which the Act of Security had not mentioned, but which now appears in the case which was being made for the Union. In Seafield's words, 'I saw no other method for securing our peace.'* This was deliberately vague. It could mean that a separate Scottish succession might lead to civil war between Jacobite and Presbyterian. It could also refer to the risk that England might invade and impose a settlement by military force, Roxburghe's 'conquest upon the first Peace'.† So far as the vote on the Treaty in the Scottish Parliament depended on rational considerations, and not on other influences, we shall see that there are good reasons to conclude that this was the most potent of all.

* *See extract 35.*   † *See extract 34.*

SIX

Volte-face

The *volte-face* was abrupt and unexpected. On 18 July 1705, the Scottish Parliament had passed the Resolve, again asserting their determination to maintain the 'independancie of this Kingdome'.* The Court then decided to abandon their attempt to persuade Parliament to accept the Hanoverian Succession and try the alternative of negotiations for a treaty. Less than two months later, on 1 September 1705, the appointment of Commissioners to conduct the negotiations came before Parliament. As we have seen, Seafield hoped, without much confidence, that it might be possible to bring influence to bear so that the nomination would be left to the Queen;† and this was in fact achieved by an extraordinary act on the part of the Duke of Hamilton, the ostensible leader of the opposition to the Union. At the end of a long meeting, when many members assumed that the day's business was over, Hamilton (who had assured his party that the question would not come to a vote that day) rose and made this very proposal. Lockhart of Carnwath, who was one of Hamilton's supporters, said that this was something which his party 'did not expect should have been   *49* moved that Night, and never at any time from his Grace, who had, from the beginning of the Parliament to this Day, roared and exclaimed against it on all Occasions; and about 12 or 15 of them ran out of the House in Rage and Despair, saying aloud, 'twas to no Purpose to stay any longer, since the Duke of Hamilton had deserted and so basely betray'd them.' The Government seized the chance and carried the resolution by eight votes. 'From this Day',   *50* Lockhart concludes, 'may we date the Commencement of Scotland's Ruine.' It meant that there would be no real negotiation but an arrangement between two groups each nominated and controlled by the Queen's English ministers.

Hamilton had such prestige and was so trusted by his followers that he was able to survive this blow to their trust, and frustrate their plans on three separate later occasions when the Treaty itself was under debate. 'All were unwilling', wrote   *51* Lockhart, 'to believe anything that was amiss of one, who had

* See extract 15. † See extract 16.

stood so firm, and done such service to his country.' Hamilton's mismanagement, or deception, of the opposition to the Union was so destructive that the modern English historian, G. M.
52   Trevelyan, described him as 'the instrument, under Heaven, of its almost miraculous passage'.

How is Hamilton's conduct to be explained? Most 19th- and 20th-century historians have attributed it to irresolution, to wavering between his political convictions and anxiety to protect his claim to the Scottish throne by descent and his English estates acquired by marriage. This theory does not agree with the impression which he made on his contemporaries. Lockhart, writing after the bitter experience of his parliamentary twists and turns, has this description:

53   'He was Master of an Heroick and Undaunted Courage: a Clear, Ready, and Penetrating Conception, and knew not what it was to be surpriz'd; having at all Times and on all Occasions his Wits about him . . . never was a Man so well qualified to be the Head of a Party, as himself, for he could with the greatest Dexterity, apply himself to, and sift thro' the Inclinations of different Parties, and so cunningly Manage them that he gained some of all to his; and if once he had enter'd into a New Measure, and form'd a Project (tho' in doing thereof he was too Cautious) did then prosecute his Designs with such Courage, that nothing could either daunt or divert his Zeal and Forwardness.'

Another sharp observer, from the opposite end of the
54   political scale, the Hanoverian agent, John Macky, wrote: ' . . . he is brave in his Person, with a rough Air of Boldness; of good sense, very forward and best for what he undertakes; ambitious and haughty, a violent Enemy; hath been very extravagant in his manner of living; but now grows covetous.'

None of this sounds like a man prone to nervous indecision. Is there an alternative explanation to suggest that his vacillation was not feeble but calculated and deliberate? There is indeed a considerable body of evidence, although historians have ignored it, to suggest that he had made a deal with the English ministers, Harley and Godolphin, to sabotage the opposition which he was pretending to lead. On 30 March 1705, Col. James Graham, who was evidently an agent of the English Government, reported to
55   Harley a conversation with Hamilton who said of the Treaty: 'he desires it as much as any man in either Kingdom and will to his power promote it.' He wanted 'to demonstrate his service and

inclinations for the Queen's Service and to give undeniable proof of it. . . . He doth desire that from my Lord [Godolphin] or you he may be fully instructed to what point his skill and service may be required, and may be plainly informed without reserve how he may be most useful.'

Hamilton then made an approach to Seafield, the Lord High Chancellor of Scotland and one of the principal agents of English policy in the country. Seafield reported to Godolphin on 24 May 1705:

'being near to Kiniel, a house of Duke Hamiltons, wher he was, *56* he sent to invite me to dine, and withal said he be honerd to see me. I went and was verie weal receaved; he said he would have been readie to have served and that he made insinuations of this and that as yet he hes not ingadged in anie measur with anie of the opposing pairtie, bot I could say no more to him bot that his onlie method to be employed suitablie to his qualitie and merit was to make the first step by concurring in the Parlament, bot, as things goes, I know not if anie thing can be expected of him. This is the sum of what past.'

Hamilton himself wrote to Graham from Holyrood on 11 September 1705, only a few days after his *volte-face*: 'Our *57* Parliament is now drawing to a close. I have done her Majesty signal service in it.'

There are many clues in the *Jerviswood Correspondence*, and clear hints that the motive was money.

Roxburghe on 12 December 1704:

'I have been told by a friend of Duke Hamilton's, and one that *58* knows him well, within this eight-and-forty hours, that if the Queen had a mind for this business, Duke Hamilton was vain and necessitous.'

Johnstone on 13 January 1705:

'I have had suspicions, but now I am certain, that Duke Hamilton is tampering by the means of Harley with the Lord Treasurer . . . he must have his debts payed.'

Johnstone on 15 February 1705:

'Duke Hamilton's friends are so gross as to intimate to great men here that he is *chambre à louer*.'

Johnstone on 6 March 1705:

'Hamilton might expect all the favour for him and his family, and what money he needed. . . . He'll be for the Treaty.'

Johnstone on 7 October 1706:

'The Whig Lords are in a bargain with Duke Hamilton, and

whatever it be, it seems to be concluded; for Sunderland has let out that Hamilton, with all his faults, must and shall be a great man: this he say'd two months agoe, but now repeats it, and affirms they have him, but only hopes they have him for the Union.'

Many other members of the Scottish Parliament succumbed to pressure and agreed to support the Union openly. Hamilton's role was more devious and damaging. He continued to pose as the leader of the opposition, and was the great popular hero in consequence; but he seems to have made a secret deal to deceive his own party. This would explain too why honours were heaped on him after the Union, an English Dukedom, both the Thistle and the Garter and appointment as Ambassador to Paris. This double role would require extraordinary political skill and ice-cold nerves, but, from the accounts of his contemporaries, this is precisely the sort of man that Hamilton seems to have been. If this is in fact what happened, and it is the only explanation which agrees with all the evidence, it must be one of the most unscrupulous but successful acts of treachery in the whole of political history.

SEVEN

The Application of Power

When the struggle was over, Defoe, who was frank when his immediate purposes did not require otherwise, wrote in 1709: 'I have been a witness to the great Transaction of the Union; I know the Warmth with which England pursu'd it; I know the Difficulty with which Scotland comply'd with it.'

In fact the English pursuit of this objective was a remarkably sophisticated exercise of power, combining the blatant and the subtle, the carrot and the stick. It was also remarkably effective and rapid. Between the decision in July 1705 to go for the Union only eighteen months elapsed before it was approved by the Scottish Parliament in January 1707. Of course, this phase was only the culmination of a sustained effort since the Revolution of 1688 to 'manage' and control the Scottish Parliament.

1. *Bribery*
Of all the methods used, the most notorious was bribery, if only because popular tradition fastened on this as the most shameful aspect of the whole transaction. The members of the Scottish Parliament who succumbed have been strongly condemned ever since. Already in 1707, an anonymous pamphleteer wrote: 'Can anything be more Treacherous and Mean than for Men to degrade their own Country, and has not the Majority of the Scotch Parliament done this effectively?'

Burns's lines are familiar:

> 'What force or guile could not subdue,
> Thro' many warlike ages,
> Is wrought now by a coward few,
> For hireling traitors' wages.
>
> We're bought and sold for English gold,
> Such a parcel of rogues in a nation!'

Sir Walter Scott was equally bitter:
'Men, of whom a majority had thus been bought and sold, forfeited every right to interfere in the terms which England insisted upon. . . . Despised by the English and detested by their

59

60

61

62

own country, . . . the Unionists had lost all freedom of remonstrance, and had no alternative left save that of fulfilling the unworthy bargain they had made. . . .' '. . . the interests of Scotland were considerably neglected in the treaty of Union; and in consequence the nation, instead of regarding it as an identification of the interests of both kingdoms, considered it as a total surrender of their independence by their false and corrupted statesmen, into the hand of their proud and powerful rival.'

Some English historians have accepted the facts realistically— Henry Hallam, for instance:

63   'The Union closes the story of the Scots Constitution. From its own nature not more than from the gross prostitution with which a majority had sold themselves to the surrender of their legislative existence, it has long been odious to both parties in Scotland'.

Scottish historians have been much more reluctant to face up to the evidence, perhaps because of a distorted sense of national pride. James Mackinnon, in one of the most careful and detailed,
64   although strongly Unionist, accounts of the Union, said: 'We are not prepared to find a large body of Scottish statesmen bartering the independence of their country at the price of a few hundred pounds each. This is a crime that no political expediency can excuse—one that, if proved, must place the Treaty of Union in the pillory of indignation of every self-respecting Scotsman.'
65   George Pryde in a more recent book said that 'the charge of bribery rests on the testimony of the disgruntled and mischief-making Jacobite, Lockhart.' In fact, the evidence is extensive and undeniable, quite apart from Lockhart's (although that, too, is well authenticated, and supported by independent documents). The Hamilton case was the most daring and Machiavellian, but it was only part of a pervasive system, politely called 'management', by which the English Administration sought to maintain control of the Scottish Parliament and, in the end, to bring about its dissolution.

The main mechanism, described by Andrew Fletcher in his speeches,* was the control in London of 'places', which meant Government posts down to quite a junior level, and 'pensions', which meant awards of money for service to the Crown. Only those who voted as the 'Court' (which meant in effect the English Government) wished could expect to benefit or to keep places
66   which they already held. 'We were obliged to let it be known,' Queensberry wrote to Carstares, 'that the King was resolved that no man that opposed him should enjoy either place or pension.'

* *See extract 3.*

In the correspondence of the time, there are innumerable examples of the system at work.

The Earl of Mar, Secretary of State, wrote on 14 November 1706 to Sir David Nairne, Secretary-Depute, and the contact with the Court in London, reporting on one of the meetings of Scottish Parliament during the debate on the Union:

'Glencairn was with us, but Buchan and Galloway were against *67* us. I can say nothing for my friend Buchan, but when it shall be thought a fit time to dispose of his place to one other I'm sure I shall say nothing against it; only if it be thought fit I wou'd recommend one other of my name and a member of Parliament who has been right all along this session to succeed him.'

Mar to Nairne again on 28 November 1706:

'My Lord Northesk has all this Parliament behaved very well. *68* He is Sherief of Angus, and wou'd gladly have it for his own life and his son's. The Commissioner desir'd me to write of it to you that you may lay it before the Queen. . . . He's a very pretty honest fellow, and this will show in the country that the Queen favours those who go into the measures of the Union, which few peers of that country do.'

As an earlier example, the Earl of Queensberry, then, as later, the Lord High Commissioner and the man chiefly responsible for carrying through the Court's policy in Scotland, wrote to Carstares on 31 July 1700:

'I must tell you one thing, which you must keep very secret; I had *69* yesterday a private message from my cousin, my Lady Marshall, by which she tells me, that she does not doubt of bringing her Lord entirely under my direction, providing that she may have leave to promise him a pension of £300 as E. Marshall. I have allowed her to do it; and, and if I had the gift in my custody, I doubt not of breaking him off from that party; and I am sure he should never receive it till I had certain proof of his sincerity: for the knowledge of its being in my power would go ten times further than all the promises I can make. . . . In short, if money could be had, I would not doubt of success in the King's business here; but the low condition of our treasury keeps many things out of my power, which otherwise I could easily compass.'

Queensberry was highly rewarded for his part in the Union with an English Dukedom and an annual pension of £3000 for life; but at a crucial moment, he too required a douceur. Johnstone wrote from London on 21 September 1706 (just before the debate on the Treaty began in the Scottish Parliament):

70   'Duke Queensberry, till two days before he left this, railed at the Lord Treasurer [Godolphin]; said he was not for the Union etc but at last a sum of money quieted him. I believe the sum of money is ten thousand pounds; the thing itself is no secret.'

It was quite common for members of Parliament to write blatant requests for places for themselves or relations in return for a promise to vote the right way. When the Duke of Argyll, then with Marlborough's army in Flanders, was asked to return to Scotland to help to carry the Union, he replied on 18 July 1706:

71   'Camp at St. Luis le Tere.—I should have receiv'd your letter before Ostend, but so it is I had it only this morning. I am extremely sorry that all my friends should desire me to doe what for aught I can as yet see I shall not be able to comply with. My Lord, it is surprising to me that my Lord Treasurer, who is a man of sense, should think of sending me up and down like a footman from one country to another without ever offering me any reward. Thier is indeed a sairtin service due from every subject to his Prince, and that I shall pay the Queen as fathfully as any body can doe; but if her ministers thinks it for her service to imploy me any forder I doe think the proposall should be attended with an offer of a reward. But I am so fare from beeing treated in this manner that I cannot obtain justice even in the army, where I doe flatter my selfe I have dun the Queen as much service, to say no more, as any body in my station. My Lord, when I have justice dun me here and am told what to expect for going to Scotland, I shall be reddy to obey my Lord Treasurer's commands. Till then I hope my friends will think it fitt I stay here, unless I have sum body put over my head; and in that cais I shall lett my Lord Marlboro give my post to sumbody, who chances to be more to his mind, which will be a very noble reward for my service and I'll goe and hear Camilla in her own country.'

The year before, Argyll had himself been Lord Commissioner and had operated the system. He wrote to Godolphin on 24 June 1705:

72   'Your Lordship may remember I told you in a note of this nature before that ten or twelve thousand pounds given to pay arrears of Pensions would have been much for the Queen's service; and as then I thought, I now find the not granting of it has lost the Queen

above twenty votes; this I only tell your Lordship to convince you
that I do not presume to offer any advice without having solid
ground for it.'

George Lockhart's contribution to the evidence is given in an
Appendix to his *Memoirs*. He explains that a commission *73*
appointed by the British Parliament in 1711 to enquire into the
public accounts uncovered correspondence, produced by Sir
David Nairne on oath, about a sum of £20 000 advanced by the
Queen on 12 August 1706, ostensibly to defray debts of the Civil
List in Scotland. At the request of Queensberry and other officers
of State in Scotland, this was done secretly, because, in the words
of their letter, it 'might probably make some noise' if the matter
became known before the debate in the Scottish Parliament. In a
second letter, they added: 'We have been obliged to give Promises
to Several Persons for a considerable part of Arrears, and without
this sum they will be disappointed, which may prove of bad Consequence.' Lockhart points out that the secret procedure enabled
the Scottish ministers to dispose of it as they pleased, and not
necessarily to those who had genuine claims on the Civil List. The
distribution was revealed in an Account produced on oath by the
Earl of Glasgow. It shows payments to members of the Scottish
Parliament, ranging from £12 325 to Queensberry 'for Equipage
and daily Allowance' down to a mere £11.2.0 to Lord Banff.

'It may be doubted', Sir Walter Scott commented, 'whether *74*
the descendants of the noble lords and honourable gentlemen
who accepted this gratification would be more shocked at the
general fact of their ancestors being corrupted, or scandalised at
the paltry amount of the bribe.' Everyone on the list except the
Duke of Atholl, who was powerful enough to be worth appeasing
in any case, voted for the Union.

There is eloquent confirmation of Lockhart's report in a
letter in the British Museum:

'May it please your Grace, *75*
You have one accompt signed by the Earle off Glasgow, how the
twenty thousand pounds advanced by my Lord Treasurer was
disposed off, wee would doe anything that is in our power, to
procure it to be reimbursed to his Lop. and for a consider part of
it, it may be done and stated upon the Equivalent. Your Grace's
Equipage & dayly allowance will amount to betwixt twelve and
thirteen thousand pounds and it is already stated as owing to your
Grace, and that being a preferable debt to most off the debts on
the civill List, my Lord Treasurer may reckon upon it, but it is

impossible for us to doe more, for what was given to the Duke of Atholl, Marquis off Tweedale, Earles off Roxburgh, Marchmont, Bellcarray, Dunmore, Cromerty and singly or evenly others in small soumes, its impossible to state these soumes without discovering this haill affair to every particular person that received any part of the money, which hath been hitherto keeped secret, and its more than probable, that they would refuse to give a signatory if they were demanded of them, so the discovering of it would be of no use, unless it were to bring discredit upon the manadgement off that parliament; and all that will be loosed is about seven thousand pounds, if your Grace please, you may Lay this befor my Lord Treasurer with that secrecy that this affair requires, wee are with all respect,

Ede 20 Jully,   May it please your Grace,
    1707   your Graces most faithfull & most
                obedient humble servant.
                SEAFIELD
                GLASGOW

your Grace may be pleased to
burn this Letter when you have
read it to my Lord Treasurer.'

(Godolphin evidently insisted on keeping the letter unburnt, because it remained with his family papers until it was sold to the Museum in 1892.)

The terms of the Treaty were themselves a form of bribe because of the ingenious arrangement of the Equivalent, a sum of money which was to serve several purposes at the same time. It was calculated as the compensation due to Scotland for accepting a proportion of the English National Debt, but as compensation also for the dissolution of the Company of Scotland. It was to be used to pay off the shareholders of the company and arrears of Government salaries and pensions, and gratuities to the Commissioners who had taken part in the negotiation of the Treaty. Since many members of Parliament stood to benefit personally from these arrangements, the inducement was obvious enough. As the money was to be collected eventually from tax revenue raised in Scotland, all this was done without cost to the English Treasury. Again, Sir Walter Scott has a comment: '. . . in fact, the Parliament of Scotland was bribed with the public money belonging to their own country. In this way, Scotland herself was made to pay the price given to her legislators for the sacrifice of her independence.'

2. *Spying, Infiltration and Propaganda*

We have already seen something of the activities of Daniel Defoe,* who was sent to Scotland as an agent by Robert Harley in October 1706, as the debate on the Union in the Scottish Parliament was beginning. In a letter to Harley on 13 September 1706, he gave his own ideas of his functions:

'However, That if my Notions are wrong, I may be Set Right by   77
your Instructions, I beg leav, tho' it be beginning at the wrong End, to Set Down how I Understand my present bussiness—as foll.

1 To Inform My Self of the Measures Takeing Or Partys forming Against the Union and Applye my Self to prevent them.

2 In Conversation and by all Reasonable Methods to Dispose peoples minds to the Union.

3 By writeing or Discourse, to Answer any Objections, Libells or Reflections on the Union, the English or the Court, Relateing to the Union.

4 To Remove the Jealousies and Uneasyness of people about Secret Designs here against the Kirk &c.

Sir I beg the Ordrs you please to give me may Mention if I am Right in my thoughts of these Things—and that you will give me as much light as possible in your farther pleasure Concerning my Conduct.'

The full text of Harley's Instructions has not survived, but enough to show that Defoe was to be more than a passive spy:

78

Instructions

1. You are to use the utmost caution that it may not be supposed you are employed by any person in England: but that you came there upon your own business, & out of love to the Country.

2. You are to write constantly the true State how you find things, at least once a week, & you need not subscribe any name, but direct for me under Cover to Mrs Collins at the Posthouse, Middle Temple Gate, London. For variety you may direct under Cover to Michael Read in York Buildings.

3. You may confidently assure those you converse with, that the Queen & all those who have Credit with her, are sincere & hearty for the Union.

4. You must shew them, this is such an opportunity that being once lost or neglected is not again to be recovered. England never was before in so good a disposition to make such large

* *See extracts 45 and 47.*

Concessions, or so heartily to unite with Scotland, & should their kindness now be slighted—

Even allowing for his probable exaggeration, he seems to have had remarkable success in infiltrating the inner circles in Edinburgh. He was accepted by a Committee of Parliament as a disinterested expert in trading and taxation questions, about which he knew a great deal, and by the Ministers of the Kirk as a zealot for their own cause. Few secret agents have such success as this. In addition, he was a propagandist of genius, writing at least six pamphlets on the Union question and keeping up a constant barrage in the pages of his newsletter, *The Review*. Of course, Defoe was not the only agent employed in this way. John Shute (afterwards the first Lord Barrington), well known as a polemicist in favour of the toleration of Dissenters, was also sent to Edinburgh to help to persuade the Presbyterian ministers to support the Union. He was rewarded for his efforts by appointment after the Union as one of the Commissioners of Customs.

Two Scotsmen who wrote pamphlets in support of the Union were also in the pay of the Administration: William Seton of Pitmedden (who also made some of the best pro-Union speeches in Parliament) and William Paterson, the chief architect of both the Darien Scheme and the Bank of England. In July 1700 Queensberry wrote to Carstares, who was at that time in London in the entourage of King William:

79 'And, if his Majesty would be pleased, in the same paper, and in the same way, to give allowance for a gratuity to Mr Paterson, of any sum not exceeding £100, I think it may be of use. He has been with me several times of late; and, as he was the first man that brought people here into the project of Caledonia, so I look upon him as the properest person to bring them off from the extravagancy of prosecuting it. I find him very reasonable upon the head; and he says, that he is now writing such things (which he has promised to shew me before they appear to any person) as I do hope may create some temper amongst them: And I doubt not but in time to be able to make a right use of him.'

Alexander Ogilvie wrote to Seafield in November 1704:

80 'Pitmedden younger pretends a great keyndnes to your Lo., and sayes most seriouslie to me that if your Lo. will obtain him a pension of one hundred pounds per annum, he will be your servant and give you a suitable returne.'

3. *Economic and Military Intimidation*

The English House of Commons responded to the *volte-face* on 1 September 1705 in the Scottish Parliament by repealing on 15 November the most objectionable clauses in their Aliens Act,* which had been the most obvious expression of economic intimidation. This was a necessary preliminary to the Union, because the Scottish Parliament was unwilling to proceed with such an ultimatum hanging over their heads; but this was not the only, or even the most menacing, of the threats. In his *History*, Defoe said of the Union that there was 'no other way left, to prevent the most bloody war that ever had been between the two nations.' Roxburghe, too, had spoken of the risk of military conquest.† Were statements like these mere rhetoric or sober statements of fact?

    At an early stage in the crisis, on 17 July 1703, Godolphin sent a gentlemanly and polite, but unmistakable, threat of military force to Seafield:

'England is now in war with France; if Scotland were in peace, and consequently at liberty to trade with France, would not that immediately necessitate a war betwixt England and Scotland also, as has been often the case before the two nations were under the same sovereign? And though perhaps some turbulent spirits in Scotland may be desiring to have it so again, if they please to consult history they will not find the advantage of those breaches has often been on the side of Scotland; and if they will give themselves leave to consider how much England is increased in wealth and power since those times, perhaps the present conjuncture will not appear more favourable for them, but on the contrary rather furnish arguments for enforcing the necessity of a speedy union between the two nations; which is a notion that I am sorry to find has so little prevalency in the present parliament of Scotland, and I hope your lordship will not be offended with me if I take the freedom to be of opinion they may possibly be sorry for it too, when the opportunity is out of their reach.

    I had not time to write so fully upon this subject by the last packet to my lord Commissioner, and therefore would desire the favour, if you please, that you would communicate this letter to him, and excuse the great freedom of it from, my Lord,

        Your lordship's most humble and obedient servant,

                      GODOLPHIN.'

81

82

---

    * *See extract 11.*
    † *See extract 34.*

On 9 September 1705 Johnstone reported from London a conversation with Godolphin:

83 'Without the Treaty, he said, there would be noe more Scottish Parliaments, but war, which he seems to be against, but the Whigs and Schutz are violentlye and avowedly for; and better now, they say, than after a peace, when France will have her hands free to assist Scotland.'

English troops were, in fact, moved to the Border during the debate on the Union in the Scottish Parliament. Nairn wrote from Whitehall to Mar on 26 November 1706:

84 'The troops on the Boarders are three regiaments of foot, and in the North of Ireland, three of horse, one of foot, and one of dragoons, and they have the necessary orders; but all relateing to this affair must be kept very private.'

Again on 10 December:

84 'There is 800 horse marched from this to the Borders by advice of the Duke of Marlborrow, for he thinks they will be more usefull than thrice there number of foot.'

The pamphleteers of the time took the possibility of war seriously enough to argue vigorously against it. Defoe in his first *Essay At Removing National Prejudices Against Union With Scotland* (May 1706) written before he left for Edinburgh and addressed to an English audience, conceded that military conquest was possible but, he maintained, undesirable:

85 'But some say, we are too strong for the Scots now, and there is no fear that ever they shall invade our Country any more; for that our Wealth and Strength is so much encreased, that we are able to crush them presently, and can always keep the War *out of our own Country*; that as we are become more powerful, the *Scots* are become weaker, as we are richer, they are poorer than ever, and therefore the Case alters . . .

. . . and tho' we flatter our selves with reducing the *Scots* by Force . . . I must beg Pardon to tell my Warlike Readers . . . they seem not at all to understand what it is *to fight with* the Scots. . . . Supposing the present happy Temper of both Nations towards a Union, should, to all our Misfortunes, go off, and end, as to me it seems inevitably necessary, in a bloody War between the Nations. . . .

If the Scots *should beat you* . . . they would be undone. If you invade Scotland, . . . *you are undone*. . . .

At the End of every War, *they shall have the better of you*, it shall cost you more to hold them, than to gain them, and more to lose them again, *than both.*'

James Hodges devoted a book to this theme, *War Betwixt the Two British Kingdoms Consider'd* (1705), a systematic analysis of the consequences for both countries of an attempt by England to impose a solution by force. He admitted that Scotland was in no position to resist attack because of the impoverishment since the Union of the Crowns and the neglect of military preparations. On the other hand, even a successful initial conquest would solve nothing, and expose England to the risks of maintaining a standing army in a hostile country. He argued for peace, 'one of the greatest Blessings on Earth', and a 'Friendly Settlement by Compact', not an incorporating Union. 'Wars betwixt these Two Nations have been the longest, the fiercest, the most bloody, and the most implacable that ever were betwixt any Two neighbouring People upon Earth.'

86

Hodges continued:

'By mutual Friendship, Peace, and afixed Good Understanding, Scotland may be very Useful to England, and England likewise to Scotland; and their United Strength, when freed from Jealousies of one another, must not only Prove a great Security to themselves against all Foreign Attempts, but also Contribute, in a much larger Measure than now, to the Support of the Liberties of Europe, and General Protestant Interest. Whereas, on the other Hand, no greater act of Imprudence, or rather Madness, can be imagin'd possible to enter into the Hearts of any People, than for either of those Two Nations to think of a War with one another, after considering, as is here clear'd, That Two Thousand Years past Experience proves, That no manner of Profit could ever be made of it on either side; and a prudent Foresight demonstrates, That nothing but Loss, and Increase of Danger, and Inconvenience to Both can ever be expected from it in time coming, go the Victory as it will.'

It seems likely that it was this work rather than his earlier pamphlet that prompted the Scottish Parliament to vote an award to Hodges,* especially as they did so in the same year as the publication of the book.

Sir John Clerk of Penicuik was a protégé of Queensberry and therefore, with some initial reluctance, a supporter of the Union. ('I had observed a great backwardness in the Parliament of

87

* *See extract 28.*

Scotland for a Union with England of any kind whatsoever . . .
the Duke of Queensberry threatened to withdraw all friendship
for me, I suffered myself to be prevailed upon.') In 1730, when
the struggle was long over, he set out his conclusion in a manu-
script, *Observations on the Present Circumstances of Scotland*,
which remained unpublished until 1965:

88   '. . . many in Scotland expected such a scene of misfortunes as
had been felt dureing the Civil Wars in the reign of King Charles
the First and in the end that the whole country would fall under
the Dominion of England by right of conquest. The Union of the
two Kingdoms was then thought of as the best expedient to
preserve the honour and liberties of Scotland and likeways the
peace of the whole island, for as the councils of Britain wou'd
then be united, the Succession wou'd naturally devolve on one
and the same person. This was the principal motive both in
Scotland and England for bringing about the Union.'

This is an aspect of the matter which has been generally
neglected by historians, although Sir Walter Scott agreed with
Clerk's view:

89   'The Scottish Act of Security, by which they refused to join in
settling the succession in the family of Hanover until their
national grievances were redressed, left the English Statesmen no
remedy but to enter into war with Scotland, or accomplish an
incorporating Union between the sister Kingdoms.'

T. B. Smith has recently reached much the same conclusion:

90   'The Scottish Commissioners in 1706 were certainly negotiating
. . . under the implied threat, if negotiation failed, of invasion by
one of the great captains of history at the head of a veteran army,
backed by the military resources of one of the most powerful
states in Europe.'

In the final analysis, there was one compelling argument in
favour of the Union: it offered peace. The alternative involved the
risk of internal disturbance encouraged by France or, more
probably, invasion from England and the imposition of worse
terms. In the depressed state of Scotland at the time, with the
recent memories of the 17th-century wars and all the signs of
English determination, it is not surprising that the resistance of
the Scottish Parliament collapsed. Bribery and 'management'
certainly contributed, but those who succumbed could argue that
they were making a rational choice in the face of unpredictable
risks.

EIGHT

The Treaty

The thirty-one Scottish Commissioners for the negotiation of the Treaty, appointed in London in accordance with Hamilton's Resolution, were all, with one exception, reliable supporters of Court policy. The exception was surprising—George Lockhart of Carnwath, one of the most determined opponents of incorporating union and a Jacobite. Lockhart himself tells us that he was astonished by the appointment and had no inclination to accept. He imagined that the English hoped to win him over because of his family relationship with Lord Wharton, a prominent English Whig. After consulting Hamilton, Fletcher and others, he agreed with reluctance to take part in proceedings which he found so distasteful, only to be able to observe the conduct of the negotiations from the inside. The account in his *Memoirs* is confirmed both by the published official record in the Acts of the Parliament of Scotland and by Mar's letters. In fact, Lockhart, although often dismissed by Unionist writers as a prejudiced Jacobite, is difficult to challenge as a witness. His convictions are evident in his vigorous vocabulary, but none of his critics have been able to contradict him on points of fact.

The proceedings were more of a *diktat* than a negotiation.* The Scottish Commissioners made a token stand for a federal solution, but in terms which showed that these were ready to give way. After this, there was little resistance, except on details. 'At the separate Meetings of the Scots Commissioners if a Difficulty was at any Time started, or an Objection made to what they were concluding, all the Answer you receiv'd was to this Purpose; ''tis true it had better be so and so, but we must not be too stiff; the English won't agree otherwise, and I'm sure you would not break the Treaty for this; and thus they proceeded all along, without having any Regard for the true Interest of their country.'

There was some haggling on the transitional fiscal provisions and on the number of the Scottish representatives in the United Parliament. The English at first proposed that there should be thirty-eight Scottish members in the House of Commons, but

See extract 31.

91

92

93

agreed finally to forty-five. England with five times the population
had 513, and Cornwall alone forty-four. The Scottish Lords lost
their automatic right to sit in Parliament, but sixteen of their
number were to be elected for each Parliament to seats in the
House of Lords.

94

The essential part of the Treaty was in the first four articles:

95

I   'THAT the Two Kingdoms of Scotland and England, shall
     upon the first day of May next ensuing the date hereof, and
     forever after, be United into One Kingdom by the Name of
     GREAT BRITAIN. . . .'

II   Provides that the Protestant Succession as defined in the
     English Act was to apply to the 'United Kingdom of Great
     Britain'.

III 'THAT the United Kingdom of Great Britain be Represented
     by one and the same Parliament to be stiled the Parliament of
     Great Britain.'

IV   'THAT all the Subjects of the United Kingdom of Great
     Britain shall from and after the Union have full Freedom and
     Intercourse of Trade and Navigation to and from any port or
     place within the said United Kingdom and the Dominions and
     Plantations thereunto belonging. And that there be a Com-
     munication of all other Rights, Privileges and Advantages
     which do or may belong to the Subjects of either Kingdom
     except where it is otherwayes expressly agreed in these
     Articles.'

In Article IX, the Treaty refers to 'that part of the United
Kingdom now called England' and similarly to Scotland, as
though England and Scotland were each to abandon their
separate existence; but it is not consistent in this respect. In effect
the English Parliament was to continue unchanged, apart from
its new name and the addition of the Scottish members. English
customs, duties and excises (apart from some transitional
exceptions) laws and regulations, coinage and weights and
measures were all to be applied to the new United Kingdom.
Apart from the Equivalent and other transitional measures, there
were however a number of important respects in which the two
countries were to remain separate. The most important of these
was the law.

Article XVIII provided
'That the Laws concerning Regulation of Trade, Customs, and
such Excises, to which Scotland is by virtue of this Treaty to be
lyable, be the same in Scotland, from and after the Union as in
England; and that all other Laws, in use within the Kingdom of

Scotland do after the Union, and notwithstanding thereof, remain the same force as before (except such as are contrary to or inconsistent with this Treaty) but alterable by the Parliament of Great Britain, With this difference betwixt the Laws concerning publick Right, Policy, and Civil Government, and those which concern private Right; That the Laws which concern publick Right Policy and Civil Government may be made the same throughout the whole United Kingdom; but that no alteration be made in Laws which concern private Right, except for evident utility of the subjects within Scotland.'

Article XIX provided that the Scottish Courts of Law should continue, but omitted to make any provision for appeals. Article XXI guaranteed the continuation of the rights and privileges of the Scottish Royal Burghs. The Act for securing the Protestant Religion and Presbyterian Church Government, 'expressly Declared to be a fundamental and essential condition of the said Treaty or Union in all time coming', guaranteed the continuation of the separate Scottish Church and educational system. In another respect, where an opportunity for reform might have been taken, the existing practice was to continue: [96]

'That all heritable Offices, Superiorities, heritable Jurisdictions, Offices for life, and Jurisdictions for life, be reserved to the Owners thereof, as Rights of Property, in the same manner as they are now enjoyed by the Laws of Scotland, notwithstanding of this Treaty.'

It was presumably this last provision, as well as the way in which the Treaty was forced through Parliament, representing only the Nobles, lairds and burgesses, which prompted Tom Nairn to say in a recent book:

'. . . there are many stateless nationalities in history, but only one Act of Union—a peculiarly patrician bargain between two ruling classes, which would have been unthinkable earlier, under absolute monarchy, and impossible later, when the age of democratic nationalism had arrived.' [97]

It was more of an imposition than a bargain, but even so the terms of the Treaty show a realistic appreciation of the political realities. If the Equivalent was a disguised bribe, the respect for the heritable jurisdictions, the Royal Burghs and the Kirk, even of the law, were all recognition of the sources of political power in Scotland and concessions to the classes and groups whose consent had to be obtained. They meant that the Treaty was much less complete in its effect than is often represented. It has been well summarised by William Ferguson: 'Scotland lost her [98] sovereignty both in theory and in practice; in theory so did England, but not in practice.' Sovereignty was certainly lost; but, especially in an age when the Church, education and the law had more effect on people's lives than governments, the separate existence of Scotland was impaired but not destroyed. The English constitutional lawyer, A. V. Dicey, and the Scottish historian, R. S. Rait, in a joint book were so enthusiastic about the Union that they described it as 'the wisest Act ever sanctioned by a Scottish or an English Parliament' but they also said: 'the supreme glory of the Act [was] that while creating the political unity it kept alive the nationalism both of England and of Scotland.'

NINE

The Reception of the Treaty in Scotland

In his first letter to Harley from Edinburgh on 24 October 1706, Defoe wrote: 'I am sorry to Tell you here is a Most Confused scene of affaires; and The Ministry have a Very Difficult Course to steer.' There was a 'Generall Aversion' to the Union. Hamilton, regarded as the main hope of resistance to it, was followed 'with Huzzas from the Parliament house quite Thro' the City', but there was a constant uproar of protest against its supporters. Defoe was nearly caught in one of these demonstrations: 'I Casually stayd at the house I went then to Till Dark and Thinking to Return to my Lodging, found the wholl City in a Most Dreadfull Uproar and the high street Full of the Rabble. . . . In This posture Things stood about 8 to 9 a Clock and the street seeming passable I Sallyed Out and Got to my Lodging. I had not been Long There but I heard a Great Noise and looking Out Saw a Terrible Multitude Come up the High street with A Drum at the head of Them shouting and swearing and Cryeing Out all scotland [*sic*] would stand together, No Union, No Union, English Dogs, and the like.'

Other observers tell the same story. Leven, the Governor of Edinburgh Castle, for example, wrote to Godolphin on 26 October about the popular enthusiasm for Hamilton:
'As they went along the streets there were repeated huzzas and acclamations of praise to his grace by those his rabble attendants. This on Wednesday last came yet to a greater height, for they not only attended the Duke of Hamilton in his coming to the House, but gave such loud huzzas when his grace entered the House as were heard by all the members when sitting on their benches.'

The tumult was not confined to Edinburgh. There were prolonged riots in Glasgow. In Dumfries the Articles of Union were burned ceremoniously. Addresses against the Union poured into Parliament from all over the country.* There was not one in favour. 'Why', wrote Nairne from London on 14 March 1706,

100

101

102

* *See, for example, extracts 29 and 41.*

'has there not been some pains taken to gett counter address from
some places?' But Mar thought it hopeless and replied: 'We
thought it better to lett them allone, for it is past time to gett
verie maney, and few wou'd look worss than non.' In Parliament,
Mar fell back on the argument that Parliament alone 'was the
fitt judge to consider of the terms of the Union.' In the same
spirit, Argyll said that the addresses 'were only fit to make kites
of'.

In his Observations of 1730, Clerk conceded that the Union
was 'disagreeable to the generality of the people', and that it was
'confirmed in the Parliament of Scotland contrary to the inclinations of at least three-fourths of the Kingdom.' All the evidence
suggests that this is a bland understatement of a nearly unanimous
reaction of dismay and aversion.

TEN

The Final Debate

The debate on the Treaty began in the Scottish Parliament on 3 October 1706 and continued until 16 January 1707, when Queensberry touched the Act with the sceptre to signify Royal assent. Unfortunately, we have no full account of the content of this long discussion. The official record in the Acts of the Parliament of Scotland is admirably succinct and lucid, but it records only what was proposed and passed, or rejected, not what was said. In his *History*, Defoe has a verbose account, taking care that the anti-Union dogs should have the worst of it; but he gives the text of only three speeches. He never mentions Andrew Fletcher. One member, Hume of Crossrig, kept a diary, but the entries are tantalisingly brief. There is a fairly full account, although highly partial and personal, in the letters of the Earl of Mar. As Secretary of State he acted virtually as Leader of the House and made it his business to keep his masters in London informed. Lockhart in his *Memoirs* gives a vivid impression of events as they appeared to the Opposition.

It is apparent from all of these accounts that the debates were tense and strongly contested, even if, according to Lockhart, the Government seldom replied to the argument, but forced each point quickly to the vote, 'having resolv'd to trust their number *107* of Led-Horses, and not to trouble themselves with reasoning'. Mar was not at first confident of success. Before the Session opened he wrote on 18 August 1706: 'We shall have pritty hard *108* work in the Parliament, but the terms of the Union are so reasonable, fair and advantageous, that if we have some time before the Parliament meet to discourse people I doubt not of gaining grownd, and the more because if the Union shou'd fail I see not what possiblie we can do to save our country from ruin.'

On 21 September he wrote to Harley: 'I cannot say we are *109* sure of success.' As soon as the House began to go through the Treaty clause by clause, however, it became apparent that the majority, constructed since the *volte-face* of 1705, was holding up. This was especially true of the nobility, the principal recipients of pensions and places. In the Scottish Parliament all three estates sat together in the same House. It was the Lords, and not the representatives of the Burghs and Shires, who, in Hume Brown's words, 'went steadily for the Union'. By 19 November Mar was able to report: 'I'm hopeful now that nothing can make the Union miscarie here but force, and it wou'd be hard if it shou'd faill so, when the plurality of the Parliament are for the thing and have alreadie past the most deficult thing of it.'

This was not achieved without long and bitter sessions. Mar's letters are full of complaints about the pressure: 'It grew at last so late and evry body faint with hunger, for most of us had eat none that day'; 'The debate upon it lasted the whole day till it was dark.' There are many references to Fletcher, whom Mar seems to have liked personally: 'I hope Salton and I shall still be in speaking terms tho' not of the same opinion in this measure of the Union.' 'A damn'd villaneous Union', Fletcher said to Mar's brother, 'and so much the more because those who pretended to carry it on were certainly against it in their minds.' In Parliament, Fletcher was not always able to control his fury that 'the wholle nation are grown rogues'. 'Today Fletcher in passion said that the Treaters [negotiators] had betray'd their trust', Mar records. Elsewhere he speaks of him running out of the House in a rage, or being in a 'vast heat'. It is very plain, despite Defoe's studied silence, that Fletcher took a very active part throughout the debate. At one point, Mar says: 'Fletcher gave us two of his study'd speeches, which certainly we'll have 'eer long in print'; but he was wrong about the printing and we have very few full texts apart from those included in Defoe's *History*.

Perhaps with malice, or perhaps because it was the only anti-Union speech in this Session which was available in print, Defoe gives the famous speech of Belhaven as his only specimen on the opposition side. It was, in its day, admired outside Parliament as a moving piece of rhetoric, but it was histrionic and emotional, and far removed from the incisive logic of Fletcher. It probably did more damage than good to his cause among the hard-headed realists in the House; but the speech was more than an emotional outburst against the pain of the loss of independence. He made some effective points against the Treaty:

'If the Lords Commissioners for England had been as civil and complaisant, they should certainly have finished a foederal treaty likewise, that both nations might have the choice, which of them to have gone into, as they thought fit; but they would hear of nothing but of an entire and complete Union, a name which

comprehends an Union, either by incorporation, surrender, or conquest; whereas our Commissioners thought of nothing but a fair, equal, incorporating Union; whether this be so or not, I leave it to every man's judgement; but as for myself, I must beg liberty to think it no such thing. For I take an incorporating Union to be, where there is a change both in the material and formal points of Government, as if two pices of metal were melted down into one mass, it can neither be said to retain its former form or substance, as it did before the mixture. But now when I consider this treaty, as it hath been explained and spoke to before us these three weeks past, I see the English Constitution remaining firm, the same two Houses of Parliament, the same taxes, the same customs, the same excises, the same trade in companies, the same municipal laws and Courts of Judicature, and all ours either subject to regulations, or annihilations: only we have the honour to pay their old debts, and to have some few persons present for witnesses to the validity of the deed, when they are pleased to contract more.
Good God! What, is this an entire surrender?'

Seton of Pitmedden, whose speech was regarded as the most effective defence of the Union, concentrated on the isolation of Scotland in an age of mercantile rivalry backed by naval power:

'With Holland we can have no advantageous alliance, because its chief branch of trade is the same with ours; with the English we can expect no profitable friendship, for they being our near neighbours, will be jealous of our increase in power; and from France few advantages can be reaped, till the old offensive and defensive league be revived betwixt France and Scotland, which would give umbrage to the English, and occasion a war betwixt them and us. And allowing the Scots, in such a juncture, with the assistance of France, to conquer England; Scotland by that conquest, could not hope to better its present state; for it is more than probable, the conqueror would make his residence in England, as formerly the northern people used to do in their southern expeditions.' *121*

He replied also to the advocates of federalism, using the argument which is still current today:
'It is true, the words, Foederal Union, are become very fashionable, and may be handsomely fitted to delude unthinking people; but if any member of this House will give himself the trouble to examine what conditions or articles are understood by these words, and reduce them into any kind of foederal compacts, whereby distinct nations have been united, I will presume to say, *122*

these will be found impracticable, or of very little use to us. But to put that matter in a clear light, these queries ought to be duly examined, whether a foederal union be practicable betwixt two nations accustomed to a monarchical government? Whether there can be any sure guaranty projected for the observance of the articles of a foederal compact, stipulated betwixt two nations, whereof the one is much superior to the other in riches, numbers of people, and an extended commerce? Whether the advantages of a foederal union do balance its disadvantages? Whether the English will accept a foederal union, supposing it to be for the true interest of both nations? Whether any foederal compact betwixt Scotland and England, is sufficient to secure the peace of this island, or fortify it against the intrigues and invasions of its foreign enemies? And, whether England, in prudence, ought to communicate its trade and protection to this nation, till both kingdoms are incorporated into one?'

123

If we know comparatively little about the arguments used in Parliament, we can deduce a good deal from the pamphlets of the time, described by Defoe as the 'pen and ink war'. He himself was by far the most prolific participant. The two leading Scottish exponents of the case for the Union, Paterson and Seton, were not very persuasive. Paterson's *An Inquiry into the Reasonableness and Consequences of a Union with Scotland* is a rambling, muddled

124

work, relying more on assertion than argument: '. . . nothing less than a Compleat Union can effectually secure the Religion, Laws, Liberties, Trade, and in a word, the Peace and Happiness of this Island.' He repeated the threat that war was the only alternative: 'Since a Civil War can never have a happy, or effectual end, but in an Union, it must certainly be better to make it by Treaty, than to stay till it comes the other way.'

Seton's *Scotland's great Advantages by a Union with England* is much less effective than his speech in Parliament (which perhaps Defoe improved in his report). He summarises the advantages of the Union as he sees them:

125

'In a word, sir, a union has been ever thought so much for the peace and safety of Britain, and so often attempted, that it's to contradict common sense, and the voice of mankind, to deny it. And therefore I apprehend the mistakes that are about it proceed from some other cause, and shall charitably suppose the opposers of it to have no other worse design and view, than that they conceive it not entirely for the advantage of Scotland. But if they will allow themselves to reason calmly, and without prejudice, they will find that if the whole island gain by it, then Scotland must have its share of the advantage, and be in a quite other condition of thriving than it is at present. No doubt England expects benefit by it, and we have no reason to grudge it, if Scotland get more than the equivalent. England secures an old and dangerous enemy to be their friend, and thereby peace at home, and in more safety to carry on designs abroad. Scotland will not be alarmed by the threatenings of a powerful and rich neighbour, nor so easily put under the yoke of a foreign enemy. England gains a considerable addition of brave and courageous men to their fleet, armies, and plantations, and we secured by their protection, and enriched by their labours. We send our commodities and useful manufactures to them, and have money or other necessaries remitted to us. They have free access to all our seas and ports, are capable of all privileges of burghers or citizens; and we the same among them, can plant colonies at a cheaper rate, and with more assurance than formerly, will see our artificers improve, and our land better cultivated and manured.'

The point about cultivation and manure may seem a strange logical jump, but it is a point made by other pamphleteers.

It was left to Defoe to carry the main weight of replying to the opponents of the Union, especially Fletcher and Hodges. Much of the argument inside and outwith Parliament was inevitably concerned with the details of the transitional fiscal arrangements, not the only respect in which one is constantly reminded of the debate over the entry into the EEC. Apart from these, and the major questions of religion, liberty and trade (discussed in Chapter Five) Defoe had three difficult points to answer.

The first of these was the Scottish preference for a loose arrangement with England, of the kind advocated by Fletcher, which would have left Scotland free to run its own affairs in its own Parliament. Why could the advantages of peace and an equitable trading relationship not be secured in this way without the sacrifice of independence? On this point Defoe could not improve on Seton's speech. It was an unrealistic question, simply because England would not accept it. Defoe summarised the argument in his *History*:

'And thus now stood the debate.—"No incorporating union," was the word:—"Let us have an Union with England with all our hearts; but no incorporation;—let us keep our Parliament,—keep

126

our sovereignty,—keep our independency,—keep our constitution; and for all the rest, we are ready to unite with you, as firmly as you can devise."

This was thought, by most, to be just reviving the former notions of a federal union, with so many inconsistent noun-substantives in their government, that had upon all occasions been found impracticable; and which would so entirely have left both nations exposed to the possibility of relapsing into a divided condition, that it could not be expected, England, whose considerations for uniting were peace, strength, and shutting a back door of continual war and confusion from the north, should communicate trade, freedom of customs in all her ports and plantations, with egress and regress of manufactures, etc. and leave the main things yet precarious and uncertain.'

Then Fletcher's point about dancing in a trap to all eternity.* How could Scotland be confident that the guarantees in the Treaty and the Act of Security for the Church would not simply be ignored by a British Parliament in which England would have an overwhelming majority? Defoe argued repeatedly, and with apparent conviction, that the Treaty was the fundamental constitution of a new entity, Great Britain, and that it could not therefore be violated without destroying the entity itself.

Again the most considered statement is in the *History*. He is replying to the Address from the Convention of Royal Burghs:†

127 '. . . and how so great a people, so clear-sighted and wary in all other cases, came at this time to run so apparently upon a plain mistake! Since, as nothing is more plain than that the articles of the Treaty, and consequently the great heads mentioned in the above address, cannot be touched by the Parliament of Britain; and that the moment they attempt it, they dissolve their own Constitution; so it is a Union upon no other terms, and is expressly stipulated what shall, and what shall not, be alterable by the subsequent Parliaments. And as the Parliaments of Britain are founded, not upon the original right of the people, as the separate Parliaments of England and Scotland were before, but upon the treaty which is prior to the said Parliament, and consequently superior; so, for that reason, it cannot have power to alter its own foundation, or act against the power which formed it, since all constituted power is subordinate, and inferior to the power constituting.'

* See extract 25.   † See extracts 29 and 41.

Or, more picturesquely, in *The Review*:

'The Union will be a sacred thing out of the Reach of Parliament;   *128*
'twill be superior to it, in its being prior in time; for all prior
Power is superior to subsequent, as the Produce is inferior to the
thing producing. . . . Whenever the Parliament of *Britain* shall
therefore infract the Union, it blows up its own Foundation, and
by Consequence destroys itself.'

Then, how was Defoe to explain away the evident hostility
of the Scottish people to the Union, as demonstrated in particular
by the flood of Addresses against it? Here he could do no better
than Mar,* the Union was the business of Parliament (although
representative of only a minute proportion of the population) and
no one else had any right to intervene: 'As to all the rest of the   *129*
People of Scotland, who have no Right to elect Representatives,
I affirm, and think the nature of the thing demonstrates it, They
can have no Right to direct those who they have no part in
constituting. . . . [They] are meddling with what they have no
Right to be meddling with, nor any way concerned in.'

It was a strange argument to be used by Defoe, the great
radical, who at a memorable moment in his career in 1701 had
asserted the rights of the people as above Parliament in *Legion's*
Memorial to the English House of Commons: 'You are not above   *130*
the People's resentments! . . . The People of England, whom you
serve . . . do REQUIRE and DEMAND.'

But Defoe was too enthusiastic a propagandist ever to allow
consistency to spoil his argument. In England, he had argued
that the Union would be no threat to the Church establishment
in England; but, he added: 'I confess I cannot speak with the   *131*
same Assurance, that there is the same Safety to the Scots'; that
the Union would open a new market to England† and that
generally: 'I must be allow'd to say, without the least Partiality,   *132*
that the Advantage is *wholly on England's Side*, whose Power is
by the Addition of *Scotland* so fortify'd, that it must be her own
Fault, if She does not make a different Figure in all the Affairs of
Europe, to what She ever did before.' In Scotland, he did not
hesitate to produce the converse of these arguments. He was
helped, no doubt, by the anonymity of the pamphlets, and by the
poor communications between London and Edinburgh.

The debate in Parliament continued against the background
not only of the pamphleteering, but of the uproar of popular
disgust towards the Union. 'I'm not verie timerous,' wrote Mar   *133*
on 19 November 1706, 'and yet I tell you that everyday here wee

* See extract 104.   *† See extract 39.*

are in hazard of our lives. Wee cannot goe on the streets but wee are insulted.' Even so, the Government pressed steadily ahead with its secure majority, resisting all proposals for delay to allow members to consult their constituents on a matter of such fundamental importance. The opponents, conscious that they represented the country at large, in desperation sought other means.

On three separate occasions these plans were frustrated by Hamilton, although he still continued to act in Parliament as though he was determined to resist the Union. Lockhart quotes one of his speeches which, he says, drew tears from many *134* members, including even some who voted for the Union: 'Shall we in Half an Hour yield what our Forefathers maintained with their Lives and Fortunes for many Ages?'

The first idea, which seemed to have arisen spontaneously in the country, was for an armed rising, with Presbyterians from the South-West and Jacobites from the North making common cause against the Union. They were to meet at the town of Hamilton and then descend on Edinburgh to 'raise the Parliament'. At the last minute, and without consulting anyone else, Hamilton sent instructions for a postponement which disrupted the whole plan.

The next proposal was that barons, freeholders and heritors (in other words those entitled to vote in elections) should assemble in Edinburgh to approve an address to the Queen to inform her *135* of the 'almost universal aversion to the Treaty' and to ask her to call a new Parliament and General Assembly of the Church. Again at the last minute, Hamilton found a way to frustrate the scheme. He proposed the addition of a clause to the address, approving the Hanoverian Succession, precisely the point which many opponents of the Union could not accept.

136 Finally, Hamilton himself urged a final effort 'at the last Hour to save the Nation, just come to the brink of Ruin.' He proposed that a Protestation should be presented and supported by all who were against the Union and that they would then in a body leave the House and not return. This proposal was received enthusiastically by his party because they were convinced that the Union could not go ahead in the face of such a demonstration. The text was said to have been drafted by the Lord Advocate, Sir James Stuart, who, although a member of the Government, could not reconcile himself to the Union. It began by claiming that Parliament had no power to destroy the Constitution, and such a measure could only be considered by a Convention of *137* Estates, 'Clothed with a more than ordinary Power and instructed with a more immediate Sense of the Nation', and continued:

'. . . and whereas many Noble and Worthy Members of this *138*
House, and the Subjects of this Nation of all Ranks and Qualities,
have generally shown an utter Aversion to any such Union, as is
contained in the Articles of Union now lying before the House,
as appears by several Protests entered in this House upon the
Fourth, Twelfth, Fifteenth, and Eighteenth Days of November
last by past, by an Address from the Commission of the General
Assembly, by several Unanimous Presbyterial Addresses, by an
Address from the Royal Burrows (the third State of the Nation)
and by an unprecedented number of Addresses subscribed by the
Generality of the Freeholders, Magistrates and Burgesses,
especially of all those Shires which had shown themselves most
early and active in the late Revolution, and declaring their
Aversion to the present Treaty of Union. . . . I do therefore, for
myself, and in the name of all those who shall adhere to this my
Protestation, Protest against this Union in the Terms of these
Articles now before this House, as manifestly tending to subvert
that Original, Fundamental and Indissolvable Constitution, by
which the People of this Ancient Kingdom are joyned together
in a Society amongst themselves. . . .'

When the day arrived for the presentation of the Protest,
Hamilton did not appear in the House and was found at home
complaining of nothing more dignified than toothache. When he
was prevailed upon to come to Parliament, he prevaricated until
the opportunity was lost. The heart went out of the opposition
and many abandoned Parliament in despair. The Government
pressed on and finally secured the passage of the Act on 16
January 1707. 'The Union', wrote Lockhart, 'was cramm'd down *139*
Scotland's Throat.'

The Treaty was put before the English Parliament only after
its approval in Scotland. It went through with little discussion and
opposition. It had passed both the House of Commons and the
Lords by 4 March, received the Royal Assent on the 6 March and
came into effect on 1 May 1707. Seafield's comment is well known:
'There's ane end of ane auld sang.' Fletcher is said to have left *140*
Scotland with the remark, 'It is only fit for the slaves who sold it.' *141*

Queensberry set out for London accompanied by his protégé,
Clerk of Penicuik, who recounts his triumphal progress as soon *142*
as he crossed the Border. When he reached Barnet, he was met by
Ministers and nobles and escorted into London by forty-six
coaches and several hundred horsemen. On 1 May, the Queen
went to St Paul's 'to give thanks for the greatest of all the victories *143*
with which God had blessed her reign.'

Postscript

On no point had Defoe been more passionate than in his repeated assurances to the Scots that they could place absolute trust in the terms of the Treaty. The Parliament of Great Britain wasted no time in showing that he was wrong. In a whole succession of measures from 1708 onwards, Parliament disregarded the Treaty, in matters of law, the rights of the Church of Scotland, taxation and trading policy, and representation in the House of Lords.

144 'Every interest of Scotland was regarded and treated purely and simply with reference to the exigencies of political parties in England. There was not a class in Scotland which had not reason to complain of a breach of the Articles of Union, and to regret that it had ever been accomplished.'

On 14 June 1708 Mar, who with Queensberry and Seafield had been one of the three chief instruments of the Court in achieving the Union in Scotland, wrote to the Queen:

145 'I think myself oblidged in duty to lett your Majestie know that so farr as I understand the inclinations and temper of the generality of this country is still as dissatisfied with the Union as ever, and seem mightily sowr'd.'

On 10 June 1711 he assured Harley, now the Earl of Oxford and Lord Treasurer:

146 'I am not yett wearie of the Union, but still think it, if rightly used, for the good of the whole island, and also that it is the only thing which can preserve Scotland, and England too, from blood and confusion; so I do not at all repent any hand I had in it, tho' I'm affraid I have fue of either side of my opinion.'

By the end of the same year, he was writing to his brother:

147 'The English, as most of the Scots are, seem to be wearie of the Union, but when they first came to think of it seriously, I doubt of their quitting with it. What seems to be the oppinion or resolution of our countrymen here for relieving us of this hardshipe is one of two, either to dissolve the Union or else an Act of Parliament reversing what is done by the House of Lordes, and putting us in the same place and condition we were before, and as we understand it. As to dissolveing the Union in a Parliamentary way, I despair of it, or if it were possible in doing it, they wou'd fix the succession, and in that case Scotland wou'd loose any aw it could have over England. . . . Thus are we situat, and I believe never were people in harder circumstances. . . . If we saw a possibility of getting free of the Union without a civill warr we wou'd have some comfort, but that I'm affraid is impossible.'

By 1713 the Scottish members of all parties determined to make an effort to dissolve the Union. Seafield (now the Earl of Findlater), who had worked so hard to accomplish the Treaty, moved a motion for its dissolution in the House of Lords. It failed by four votes.

List of Sources

Short Titles

A.P.S.—Acts of the Parliament of Scotland (1824); Vol. XI

Carstares *Papers—State Papers and Letters Addressed to William Carstares*; edited by Joseph McCormick, Edinburgh, 1774

Defoe *History*—Daniel Defoe: *The History of the Union Between England and Scotland* (London, 1786)
> *Letters—The Letters of Daniel Defoe*, ed G. H. Healey (1969)
> *Review—The Review of the State of the English Nation* (Periodical)

Fletcher *Political Works—The Political Works of Andrew Fletcher of Saltoun* (Edition of 1749, Glasgow)

H.M.C.—Reports of the Historical Manuscripts Commission

Jerviswood *Correspondence*—George Baillie of Jerviswood: *Correspondence, 1702-1708.* Bannantyne Club Vol. 72 (1842)

Lockhart *Memoirs—Memoirs Concerning the Affairs of Scotland from Queen Anne's Accession to the Throne to the Commencement of the Union of the Two Kingdoms of Scotland and England in May 1707* (London, 1714) (There is a later 'authorised' edition, London 1817; but the page references are to the earlier one.)

Mar and Kellie *Papers*—H.M.C. Report on the Manuscripts of the Earl of Mar and Kellie (1904)

Seafield *Letters—Letters Relating to Scotland in the Reign of Queen Anne by James Ogilvy, first Earl of Seafield, and others.* Edited by P. Hume Brown. S.H.S. 2nd series, Vol. XI (1915)

S.H.S.—Publications of the Scottish History Society

Chapter One

1 Polydore Vergil *Historia Anglica*, Vol. II, *pp 1539–1540*
   [Quoted by R. L. Mackie: *King James IV of Scotland* (Edinburgh 1958) *p 93*]
2 T. B. Macaulay *History of England* (London, 1858), Vol. III, Chapter 13 *pp 253–254*
3 Fletcher *Political Works pp 195–199*
4 Seafield *Letters pp 180–181*
5 Fletcher *Political Works pp 274–276*
6 Defoe *History pp 50 and 74*

Chapter Two

7 George Ridpath *The Proceeding of the Parliament of Scotland, 1703, Preface*
8 A.P.S. Vol. XI *pp 136 and 137*
9 Jonathan Swift *The Publick Spirit of the Whigs* in *Political Tracts*, 1713–1714 (Oxford, 1953) *p 49*

10   Sir John Clerk of Penecuik   *Observations on the Present Circum-stances of Scotland.* S.H.S. 4th series, Vol. 2. Miscellany X (1965) *p 190*

Chapter Three

11   Cobbett's   *Parliamentary History* 3, Anne 1704, Vol. VI *Columns 372–374*
12   Defoe   *History p 86*
13   H.M.C.   Report XIV, Appendix Part III (M.S.S. of Countess Dowager of Seafield) *pp 194–195*
14   Seafield   *Letters p 49*
15   ibid   *p 61–62*
16   ibid   *p 60*
17   H.M.C.   Report XIV Appendix Part III *pp 206–207*
18   Seafield   *Letters p 62*
19   McIlwain (ed)   *The Political Works of James I* (1918) *pp 271–273* [Quoted by Ferguson (See Note 94) *p 100*]
20   Defoe   *History p 17*
21   J. A. Froude   *History of England from the Fall of Wolsey to the Defeat of the Spannish Armada* (1873) *p 5*
22   Fletcher   *Political Works p 293*
23   ibid   *pp 281–282*

Chapter Four

24   Fletcher   *Political Works p 318*
25   Andrew Fletcher   *State of the Controversy Betwixt United and Separate Parliaments* (1706) *pp 25, 4, 16*
26   ibid   *p 6*
27   James Hodges   *The Rights and Interests of the Two British Monarchies* (1703) *pp 3, 6, 34, 35*
28   A.P.S.   Vol. XI *p 221*
29   Text printed as Appendix X (*p 613*) in Defoe's *History*
30   Mar and Kellie   *Papers p 242*
31   Carstares   *Papers p 743*

Chapter Five

32   Jerviswood   *Correspondence p 138*
33   ibid   *p 97*
34   ibid   *p 28*
35   Seafield   *Letters p 63*
36   H.M.C.   Vol. XIV Appendix Pt III *p 157*
37   James Hodges   op. cit. *p 26*
38   Fletcher   *Political Works p 283* et seq.
39   Defoe   *Review* Vol. III No. 119 Oct. 5, 1706 *p 474*
40   Defoe   *History*, Dedication to Queen Anne
41   as No. 28
42   Defoe   *Review* Vol. III, No. 131, 2 Nov 1706 *p 522*

43   Lockhart   *Memoirs p 282*
44   Mar and Kellie   *Papers p 315*
45   Defoe   *History p 95*
46   A.P.S.   Vol. XI *pp 402–403*
47   Defoe   *Letters pp 173 and 159*
48   ibid   *p 226*

Chapter Six

49   Lockhart   *Memoirs p 170*
50   ibid   *p 172*
51   ibid   *p 173*
52   G. M. Trevelyan   *England Under Queen Anne:* Vol. II—*Ramillies and the Union with Scotland* (1932) *pp 224–225*
53   Lockhart   *Memoirs p 30*
54   John Macky   *Memoirs* (1733) *p 178*
55   H.M.C.   15th Report App. Pt IV (1897) *p 171*
56   Seafield   *Letters p 46*
57   H.M.C.   10th Report App. Pt IV (1885) *p 340*
58   Jerviswood   *Correspondence pp 22, 35, 47, 55, 162*

Chapter Seven

59   Defoe   *Review* Preface to Vol. V
60   'Vulpone'   *Remarks on Some Proceedings in Scotland Relating both to the Union and Protestant Succession Since the Revolution, In a Letter to a Member of Parliament* (1707) (N.L.S. MG 1559 C. 31 (5)) *p 28*
61   Robert Burns   Oxford Standard Authors Edition (ed. James Kinsley) *p 512*
62   Sir Walter Scott   *Tales of a Grandfather* (edition of 1889; edited F. W. Farrar) *p 770*
63   Henry Hallam   *The Constitutional History of England* (7th edition, 1845) Vol. III *p 336*
64   James Mackinnon   *The Union of England & Scotland* (1907) *p 343*
65   George Pryde   *The Treaty of Union of Scotland and England, 1707* (1950) *p 31*
66   Carstares   *Papers p 401*
67   Mar and Kellie   *Papers p 321*
68   ibid   *p 338*
69   Carstares   *Papers p 585*
70   Jerviswood   *Correspondence p 160*
71   Mar and Kellie   *Papers p 270*
72   Duke of Argyll   (J. D. R. Campbell) ed. *Intimate Society Letters of the 18th Century* (1910) Vol. I *p 26*
73   Lockhart   *Memoirs pp 405–420*
74   Scott   op. cit. (Note 62) *p 769*
75   British Museum   Add. MSS. *34, 180*
76   Scott   op. cit. *p 769*

77 Defoe *Letters pp 126–127*
78 ibid *p 132*
79 Carstares *Papers pp 583–586*
80 Seafield *Correspondence from 1685 to 1708*, ed. James Grant S.H.S. New Series. Vol. III (1912) *p 382*
81 Defoe *History p 64*
82 H.M.C. Report XIV Appendix Part III *p 198*
      Text also in J. M. Graham: *Annals and Correspondence of the Viscount and 1st and 2nd Earls of Stair* (1875) Vol. I *pp 380–381*
83 Jerviswood *Correspondence, p 122*
84 Mar and Kellie *Papers pp 336 and 353*
85 Defoe *First Essay*, etc. *pp 20, 21, 22*
86 Hodges *War Betwixt*, etc. *pp 22, 4, 20*
87 Sir John Clerk of Penecuik *Memoirs* S.H.S. Vol. 13 (1891), *p 58*
88 Sir John Clerk of Penecuik *Observations on the Present Circumstances of Scotland* (1730) (See Note 10) *p 191*
89 Sir Walter Scott's edition of Lord Somer's *Tracts* (2nd Ed. 1814). Note on page 510 of Vol. XII
90 T. B. Smith *The Union of 1707 as Fundamental Law* in *Studies Critical and Comparative* (1962) *p 9*

Chapter Eight

91 Lockhart *Memoirs pp 187, 188*
92 ibid *p 207*
93 ibid *p 210*
94 William Ferguson *Scotland's Relations with England: A Survey to 1707* (1977) *p 236*
95 A.P.S. Vol. XI *pp 406–414*
96 ibid *p 414*
97 Tom Nairn *The Break-up of Britain: Crisis and Neo-Nationalism* (1977) *p 129*
98 William Ferguson op. cit. (Note 94) *p 240*
99 A. V. Dicey and R. S. Rait *Thoughts on the Union Between England and Scotland* (1920) *pp 355 and 353*

Chapter Nine

100 Defoe *Letters pp 133–135*
101 Duke of Argyll op. cit. (Note 72) Vol. I *p 50*
102 Mar and Kellie *Papers p 320*
103 ibid *p 328*
104 ibid *p 324*
105 Lockhart *Memoirs p 235*
106 Clerk *Observations* (See Note 10) *pp 193, 192*

Chapter Ten

107 Lockhart *Memoirs p 222*

108   Mar and Kellie   *Papers p 272*
109   ibid   *p 281*
110   P. Hume Brown   *History of Scotland* (1909) Vol. III *p 112*
111   Mar and Kellie   *Papers p 328*
112   ibid   *p 309*
113   ibid   *p 327*
114   ibid   *p 272*
115   ibid   *p 273*
116   ibid   *p 294*
117   ibid   *p 306*
118   ibid   *p 349*
119   ibid   *p 309*
120   Defoe   *History pp 326–327*
121   ibid   *p 314*
122   ibid   *p 315*
123   ibid   *p 75*
124   op. cit.   *p 154*
125   op. cit. in Somer's *Tracts*, edited by Sir Walter Scott (1809–15)
          Vol. XII *p 521*
126   Defoe   *History p 232*
127   ibid   *p 246*
128   Defoe   *Review*. Vol. III, No 131, 2 Nov 1706 *p 523*
129   Defoe   *A Fourth Essay at Removing National Prejudices; with
          Some Reply to Mr Hodges and Some Other Authors who have
          Printed their Objections against An Union with England* (1706)
          p 7
130   Quoted in James Sutherland   *Defoe* (1937) *pp 71–72*
131   Defoe   *First Essay at Removing National Prejudices*, etc, (1706)
          p 16
132   ibid   *pp 26 and 27*
133   Mar and Kellie   *Papers p 329*
134   Lockhart   *Memoirs p 252*
135   ibid   *p 287*
136   ibid   *p 293*
137   ibid   *p 298*
138   ibid   *pp 299–300*
139   ibid   *p 224*
140   ibid   (1817 edition) Vol. I *p 223*
141   G. W. T. Omond   *Fletcher of Saltoun* (1897) *p 139*
142   Clerk   *Memoirs* (See Note 87) *pp 67–68*
143   Trevelyan   op. cit. (See Note 51) *p 285*

      Postscript
144   Hume Brown   *History of Scotland*, Vol. III *p 145*
145   Mar and Kellie   *Papers p 447*
146   ibid   *p 490*
147   ibid   *pp 492 and 494*